INTERVIEWING

A GUIDE FOR JOURNALISTS AND WRITERS

Gail Sedorkin and Judy McGregor

ALLEN&UNWIN

First published in 2002

Allen & Unwin
83 Alexander Street
Crows Nest NSW 2065
Australia
Phone: (61 2) 8425 0100
Fax: (61 2) 9906 2218
Email: info@allenandunwin.com
Web: www.allenandunwin.com

National Library of Australia
Cataloguing-in-Publication entry:

Sedorkin, Gail.
Interviewing: a guide for journalists and writers.

Bibliography.
Includes index.

ISBN 978 1 86508 701 6

1. Interviewing in journalism. 2. Interviewing—Technique.
3. Interviewing in mass media. 4. Interviewing on television.
I. McGregor, Judy. II. Title.

070.43

Set in 10.5/13 pt Garamond Book by Midland Typesetters
Printed and bound by SRM Production Services Sdn Bhd, Malaysia

10 9 8 7 6 5 4

CONTENTS

Acknowledgements iv

Introduction v

1. The interview . . . revealing all 1

2. Research 20

3. Getting started 37

4. Breaking the ice 56

5. The questions 68

6. Print interviews 94

7. Broadcast interviews 110

8. Telephone and email interviews 131

9. Using the information 142

10. Keeping safe 160

Resources 175

Index 181

ACKNOWLEDGEMENTS

My first thanks must go to my sister Lisa, who researched, proofed, supported and encouraged me, together with Barbara Alysen and Debra McCoy, my husband Nick, my mother and father, Mollie and Lou Svanetti, and brother Andrew. A special thanks to NZ colleague Jim Tully, who helped to get the project off the ground and assisted with one of the initial chapters, to Deakin colleagues John Tidey and Mandy Oakham and, from around Australia, Roger Patching, Mina Roces, Lindsay Simpson and Belinda Weaver.

For their time and expertise I would like to thank Ian Baker, Peter Bennetts, Craig Borrow, Andrea Carson, Peter Davis, Clive Dorman, Jon Faine, Liz Gray, John Hamilton, the *Herald Sun*, Sharon Hill, Dorothy Horsfield, Louise Keller, the late Paul Lyneham, Susan Mulholland, Kerry O'Brien, Network Nine, SBS Publicity and Andrew Urban.

And, of course, at Allen & Unwin, Elizabeth Weiss, who kept the project going, Emma Cotter, for her patience, and Emma Sorensen and Karen Young for their support.

Gail Sedorkin

To John Harvey, with love.

Special thanks to Jim Hubbard for permission to use his cartoon and to Dr Brian Edwards and Al Morrison for their time and insights.

Judy McGregor

INTRODUCTION

Almost every journalist has a horror story, or two, to tell about their first interviewing attempts—failing to ask questions, not listening to the answers, a tape recording with no sound, or returning to the newsroom practically empty-handed are common disasters.

David Leser says that his first interview 22 years ago, when he was working for *The Daily Telegraph* as a cadet journalist, is still etched in his brain:

> It was my first day on the job and there was an industrial dispute and I had to call management and workers to get a response. This was my very first call for my very first story and I was so nervous that, when the person answered the phone, I promptly forgot not only whom I was calling but why I was calling (2001:8).

Cadets' interview training often consisted of watching a senior reporter for a few days before being let loose to sink or swim, despite the fact that interviewing is an integral part of journalism and professional writing. In fact, Ken Metzler believes that 'good reporting is about 80 per cent interviewing', and goes on to ask, 'What is the point of being a good writer if you have nothing of substance to convey through your writing?' (1977: 133).

Bob Jervis agrees that 'interviewing is the most important,

and the most difficult, skill of the journalist'. It takes the 'average cadet . . . about eight weeks to become a reasonably adept intro-writer; about a year to learn to structure a fairly complicated news story passably; and much, much longer to become a competent interviewer' (1989: 96).

There's no more daunting prospect than having to meet with a total stranger, for the sole purpose of eliciting information from them on a topic you know little to nothing about. Interviewing ranks on the stress levels right up there with giving a one-hour speech to a crowded room but, as with giving a speech, there are three keys to success:

1. preparation;
2. preparation; and
3. preparation.

Masterton and Patching sum it up in just one line: 'In every case the best interviews are those that are best prepared, with the best questions in the best sequence, and where the reporter listens carefully to every word of every answer' (1997: 202).

This is the main point we are making in this book, and it is stressed again and again in the tips, checklists and advice provided by some of the best interviewers from Australia and New Zealand. Cadets, trainees and students were also canvassed about their major fears, and we hope that they will find answers to their questions in these pages.

Organise your contact book (which will quickly become your bible), let our research tips guide your own digging, adapt our questions to your topic and incorporate our step-by-step guide to each and every interview you conduct. Following the best practice guidelines in this book will allow any writer to craft superior stories from quality interviews.

To make the most of your interviews, however, enjoy the incredible opportunity you have to talk to so many interesting people!

REFERENCES

Jervis, B. 1989, *News Sense*, Advertiser Newspapers Limited, Adelaide

Leser, D. 2001, 'The interview: art or a confidence trick?' *The Walkley Magazine*, issue 13: p. 8

Masterton, M. and Patching, R. 1997, *Now the News in Detail*, Deakin University Press, Geelong

Metzler, K. 1977, *Creative Interviewing: The Writer's Guide to Gathering Information by Asking Questions*, Prentice-Hall Inc., New Jersey

THE INTERVIEW ...
REVEALING ALL

Bashir: Did your relationship go beyond a close friend-
          ship?
Diana: Yes it did, yes.
Bashir: Were you unfaithful?
Diana: Yes, I adored him. Yes, I was in love with him.
          But I was very let down (http://www.bbc.co.uk/
          politics97/diana/panorama.html).

The two questions and the dramatic answers came from one of the most talked-about media interviews of our times. The 1-hour interview with the late Diana, Princess of Wales and BBC1's Martin Bashir was viewed by millions of people around the world. The 'Panorama' interview was promoted as one in which Princess Diana 'talked openly about her life, her children, her failed marriage, her eating disorders and depression, her husband's relationship with Camilla Parker-Bowles and her own infidelity' (http://www.pbs.org/wgbh/pages/frontline/shows/royals/interviews/bbc.html).

Today interviews, particularly those broadcast on television, can attract very large audiences. But what is an interview? Is it a conversation between two people or an exchange where one person challenges the other; a way of tricking people into revealing facts or an argument where two opponents are pitted against each other? Is it an opportunity for the interviewee to give a speech; or is a journalist merely a conduit for channelling information from the source to the public? It could easily be argued that interviewing is all of these, and more. Today an interview can be anything from a rapid exchange to get a small 'grab' or 'soundbite' (an answer or part of an answer that can be as short as one second for broadcast); to a lengthy feature interview where the whole exchange—questions and answers—are published or broadcast. Highly respected Australian journalist Geraldine Doogue says the interview is 'a conversation above all . . . a disciplined conversation . . . where you're trying hard, as opposed to a rambling chat, and a conversation where you get beyond the obvious' (ABC Radio, February 1999).

A popular definition of interviewing is that it is a conversation with a purpose—to inform, entertain and challenge audiences. Bell and van Leeuwen note in *The Media Interview* that 'interviews are now seen as the most natural and obvious way of gathering and disseminating information' (1994: 2). The interview is the main way that journalists collect information for news stories. The better the interview, the better the information and the stronger the story. Interviewing is an integral skill for the journalist and one that is difficult to master.

All interviews are different. They may involve trying to elicit opinion or emotion, or just gathering fact. Author of *The Electronic Reporter*, Barbara Alysen, makes a distinction where 'the *tone* of the interview will also vary, from hard, to soft, to emotional . . . Reporters are also called upon to conduct *emotional* interviews such as those with the victims of crime or accidents, or their relatives' (2000: 130 original emphasis).

Mainstream news media rely on fact and opinion interviewing, and magazine journalism uses human interest interviewing for soft news and feature pieces. On the other hand newer media formats are rewriting traditional definitions to respond to technological imperatives and changes in public taste and consumer patterns.

Fact and opinion interviews relate more to hard news, while the human interest interview is used for soft news or feature pieces. The *fact* interview usually concentrates on the Who, What, When and Where questions and is used for print news briefs and broadcast news stories, where space and time are limited. The interview for *opinion* or *comment* emphasises the Why and How questions, and is more commonly used in longer stories. As Masterton and Patching note: 'A journalist wit is supposed to have said that while the broadcast news reporter chases fire engines, the current affairs reporter is down at the fire station talking to the fire chief about how to improve the service' (1997: 239). The *human interest* interview also includes *fact* and *opinion* questions, but concentrates on the emotions and the soft news angle (as in the interview with Princess Diana).

Radio New Zealand's political editor, Al Morrison, describes the different styles of interview—particularly for radio. These are: the interview for a 1-second soundbite; the interview for audio drop-ins; the continuous interview to get a 1-minute chunk; and the background interview that might never go to air (personal interview with Al Morrison, August 2000). The *Oxford Dictionary* defines the interview as 'a conversation between a reporter etc. and a person of public interest, used as a basis of a broadcast or publication' with its French form *entrevue* derived from 's'entrevoir "see each other"' (1997: 699). However not many interviews are conducted *s'entrevoir*—face-to-face—today. Tighter deadlines and generally smaller newsrooms have resulted in fewer of these 'meetings'.

Journalists, particularly electronic journalists, are increasingly reliant on telephone interviews, media conferences, doorstop interviews (where you catch someone as they are leaving another appointment), as well as email and satellite interviews.

TYPES OF INTERVIEWS

Vox pops

Vox pops (*vox populi:* voice of the people) are used regularly by print and broadcast journalists and have the benefit of immediacy and spontaneity. Essentially they are street surveys to canvass people's feelings about a person's actions or a topical issue. For instance, numerous vox pops have been conducted on smoking in public and on the popularity of political leaders. The question should be short, easily understood and 'open' (that is, the question should elicit more than a yes/no response). Everyone who is interviewed should be asked the same question to ensure the validity of the results.

Doorstops and ambushes

There are some drawbacks to spontaneity and the doorstop method is one that should be used with great care to gain an interview. A doorstop interview in which the interviewee is asked to respond to accusations or allegations of serious mis-behaviour is usually an adversarial situation. The interviewee can be inexperienced and at a disadvantage when appearing on television. In New Zealand, the Broadcasting Standards Authority (BSA) dealt with a complaint from an individual approached by a reporter and camera crew as he collected the newspaper from the mailbox in the early morning. The BSA stated that doorstop interviews should not normally be used unless every alternative way of getting the interview has been pursued even though it is not always a breach of codes of broadcasting practice.

Doorstops are now used regularly—but not always as an aggressive technique. It is sometimes the easiest way for journalists to catch busy sources when they are on their way to, or from, an appointment. For instance, you may catch a politician after a media conference or a celebrity leaving a concert or launch. Television journalists regularly use this technique, and in fact may doorstop an interviewee as they leave another media interview. Often doorstop interviews will be pre-arranged.

Deathknocks

Deathknocks are interviews where the journalist knocks on the door of relatives and friends of someone who has just died to talk to them about the deceased for a story. Print and electronic journalists are expected to do deathknocks which can be a difficult part of the job, particularly for cadets. Sharon Hill, editorial staff manager at Nationwide News, says their reporters are trained to conduct deathknocks politely and carefully. 'The fact is our journalists are very rarely turned away. People actually do want to talk about their loved one, and a story in the paper—so long as it is accurate and positive—is a great comfort to them.' She has developed a number of hints to deal with this sort of interview. They include:

- Put your notebook and pen in your back pocket. It's threatening to open a door and see a stranger with pen and notebook poised.
- Always introduce yourself.
- Check details with the family as information from the police can be wrong.
- Use open body language and try to behave as any other professional who comes into contact with a family when

someone has died suddenly. The police, the ambulance, solicitors and funeral directors are all part of the process, and so, often, are journalists (personal interview with Sharon Hill, November 2000).

Rounds and events

The work of the journalist can be roughly divided into three main 'beats' or events which include: general or daily rounds; managed events; and spontaneous or on-the-spot events. These all involve different interview contexts.

General rounds involve interviewing sources such as police, fire and ambulance services several times a day—usually by telephone. This round is often given to cadets, or less experienced reporters, and while it may seem tedious, can result in some of the best stories and leads. Please do not be discouraging in your questioning like the cadet who used to ask: 'You don't have any news for me, do you?'. Not all rounds are daily. For instance, in Far North Queensland one round involves annually calling the local wildlife park to find out if the crocodiles are nesting (a sign that the wet season is on the way), and in New Zealand rural reporters compete each year to file the first spring lamb story on the wires.

Managed events include media conferences and launches and are a common source of information for journalists today. The managed event is ideal for the organisers, giving them the opportunity to disseminate information to a large number of people at one time—a 'group interview'. One of the few advantages for the journalist is the chance to ask questions of a person who ordinarily would be impossible to catch on a one-to-one basis. The journalist can also use the answers to other journalists' questions in their story.

On the other hand there is no opportunity for an individual reporter to get a scoop, or an exclusive, when they ask their questions in public. The organisers may allow individual time at the end for journalists, but generally it is a matter of trying to conduct a doorstop as they leave if you want to ask a question solely for your own benefit.

Spontaneous events can include anything from allegations of corruption to disasters and accidents. They offer the most interesting interviews and often supply the best stories, but are generally the most difficult situations for journalists because of the lack of preparation time.

INTERVIEW STYLES

Journalists use different styles or approaches (genres). These can range from the aggressive interviewer who argues with the interviewee at every point, to the interviewer who is overawed by the 'talent', agreeing with every word and allowing the interviewee to remain unchallenged. ABC Radio's Jon Faine sees the interview as a 'contest of ideas' to test the interviewees' points of view.

> I'll adopt an adversarial approach and from one day to the next and from one hour to the next I may argue opposite points of view. If you interview the man from the bank on the day of the tellers' strike, I might put to him all the union's arguments, and then five minutes later I might be interviewing the union rep and I'll put to him all the employer's arguments. What I'm doing is I'm trying to test their points of view. And in order to put their point of view to the test I have to understand the opposite point of view and be able to follow it up (personal interview with Jon Faine, June 2000).

Other styles include the conversation and the challenge. Highly respected Australian political journalist Kerry O'Brien

Kerry O'Brien, courtesy of the Australian Broadcasting Corporation.

uses the challenge style for most of his interviews. The following segment was taken from a television interview he conducted on 15 May 2000 on the ABC's current affairs program 'The 7.30 Report' with IOC Vice-President Kevan Gosper. Gosper had been publicly accused of nepotism for allowing his daughter Sophie to be the first Australian to run with the Olympic torch in Greece. After a brief introduction Kerry does not waste any time getting to the point with his first question.

Kerry O'Brien: Kevan Gosper, you've acknowledged an error of judgement, how serious an error?

Kevan Gosper, IOC Vice-President: It's serious for me, because I allowed my personal feelings towards my daughter and I guess in my Olympic heart, to make a wrong call and I regret that and I've tried to express my apology as sincerely as I can ...

Kerry O'Brien: I have to ask—why did it take so long for you to realise the error of judgement?

. . .

Kerry O'Brien: Did it occur to you that the Greeks might

have been currying favour with you as a very powerful individual inside the IOC . . . given the problems that they're having in preparing for the 2004 Olympics?

Kevan Gosper: The fact is it never entered my mind.

. . .

Kerry O'Brien: It sounds like you're still not absolutely convinced it was the wrong thing, rather than it's wrong because of the way it was perceived. Isn't it true, though, that the only reason Sophie was invited—given that privilege—is because you were her father?

(http://www.abc.net.au/7.30/stories/s126909.html).

THE SOURCES

Journalists must be adept at a number of skills to conduct an interview. While others can help with writing the story, you're generally on your own for the interview. Journalists must decide how the interviewee is feeling about the interview and match their style accordingly. If the interviewee is looking apprehensive, the reporter may not start the interview with the toughest question. Journalists often modify their approach according to their 'talent'. For instance, they would not use the same interviewing style in an exchange with a politician, as they would when interviewing a young sportsperson.

Bell and van Leeuwen agree that the media interview can take on many forms including where 'interviewers talk to politicians in the voice of the interpellator; to experts in the voice of the student; to ordinary people in the voice of the social researcher or the counsellor; to children in the voice of the parent or teacher; to "deviant" interviewees in the voice of the interrogator' (1994: 22). Not only are there different interview types and styles, the subject of the interview has a critical effect on its outcome.

For this reason it is common for broadcast journalists to use a limited number of sources that they know are 'good talent' because they have proven to be articulate and concise. These sources are often called 'talking heads', or as Barbara Alysen describes them in *The Electronic Reporter*, 'the usual suspects'. She says 'the result is that the same speakers are seen and heard again and again. It becomes boring and it's unrepresentative' (2000: 144). A journalist's range of contacts should be broadened by asking current sources for names of anyone else who could be interviewed on the same subject.

Politicians and CEOs

These interviewees are placed together in a category, as they use the media regularly to get their message out, and are generally the most adept at handling interviews. Political and business leaders are eager to take advantage of any free space or air time. They are generally well versed in how to manage the media and deal with tough interviews, and often use public relations people as conduits. Before challenging any of this group in an interview, it is crucial to be armed with all the facts and to have researched what's been said before. Reporters need to be willing to persist and insist on answers to crucial questions. A skilled interviewer will overcome avoidance and evasion of tough questions.

Celebrities/sports stars

Celebrities, such as movie, music and sports stars, have something to sell and need the media to do this. However, they can also be quite overwhelming to the novice interviewer. Clive Dorman of Melbourne's *Age* newspaper believes a useful technique to overcome this 'awe' is to always use their first name—in other words, be familiar. Familiarity, he says, 'establishes the interview on an equal footing, where the interviewee is giving answers, rather than pronouncements' (personal interview with Clive Dorman, June 2000). Celebrities have been interviewed frequently and are often bored with the process, so it is important to develop some original questions.

The innocents

There are many interviewees who unwittingly become the focus of the media, or must participate in interviews because of their position, their actions or actions of others that impact on them. Generally journalists can distinguish people who are 'sources for the moment' and modify their approach accordingly. For example, obviously a journalist would approach survivors of a train crash with more sensitivity than a hardened criminal who has been sentenced for committing a major crime.

Criminals

It is important to be as objective as possible when interviewing criminals—showing neither empathy nor condemnation. This can be very difficult in cases that involve an interviewee who has committed a heinous crime. Journalists must distance themselves to approach these interviews.

Children

Young people are perhaps the most difficult to interview— particularly on air. Common ground should be established before the interview goes live. This may include asking about school, sports, movies or hobbies. Codes of ethics or statements of principles guiding journalists and broadcasters generally refer to the way in which reporters should deal with children in sensitive interviews. Caregivers' permission to conduct the interview is usually required when children are 16 years of age or under.

Not in the 🇬🇧 US.

Experts

Australian freelance journalist Peter Davis knows that inter-viewing experts can be a real challenge—especially when their expertise is way out of your own field. He's found a simple way to overcome these difficulties.

> I once had to interview a whole lot of physicists about cold fusion technology. They may as well have been speaking Swahili for all I knew. But I asked each one of them the same question: 'How would you explain that to someone who has never studied physics?'. Without exception, they all came up with some wonderful quotes that even I could understand (personal interview with Peter Davis, June 2000).

TOP TECHNIQUES

Whether for hard or soft news, managed or spontaneous events, you must be interested in your interviewee—and show it. The best techniques for handling interviews from some of the best interviewers have been included here.

Preparation

Kerry O'Brien believes whether you're just starting out in journalism or whether you've been in the game for 30 years, preparation is enormously important.

The more you know about the topic, the issue, or the person—the better off you are. I don't have any particular tricks in the way I do interviews, I simply endeavour to understand as much as I can by way of background reading on the subject. I try to focus in on its essential elements. What are the things that the public would really want to know about this? Which are the most interesting and compelling aspects? The more ignorant you are about either the person or the issues, the more it will show up—it's very hard to hide that. You'll often find that busy people, important people, people with pressures on their lives and on their time, will get very impatient very quickly if they feel you're stuffing them around and you don't really know what you're on about. But regardless of what their attitude is to you, you should at least have respect enough for your readers, or your audience, to do as much preparation as you can to understand the topic in advance (personal interview with Kerry O'Brien, November 2000).

Eye contact

The top tip from Australian print and broadcast journalist Andrew Urban involves the use of body language, and more specifically 'eye contact'.

My eyes don't move. I don't get easily distracted, even when we're talking on the street with cars going past, people jumping around behind the person I'm talking to, and children crying. I focus solely on the subject. I constantly listen for any clue while trying to work out the next question. It can be very difficult and very draining—but it works (personal interview with Andrew Urban, April 2000).

Atmosphere

Journalists usually try to create a comfortable atmosphere for the interviewee—even if they have to destroy this later in the interview by asking the tough question. Andrew Urban believes what journalists want most from an interview is a revelation given only to them, and that there are a number of ways to ensure that this 'revelation' occurs.

> I want to make sure people are comfortable, are not threatened. I am not confrontational—I believe the honey gets the ants. I think it's the approach—a lot of information is given in the start of the interview. Journalists should be sceptical—not cynical. If you're cynical you've limited what you're going to get—you need the luxury of being objective. If you have cynicism and preconceptions about what you want to do, if you want a particular outcome, it's a disincentive for the person to open up. The key thing for me is finding the story—you won't find the story if you have blinkers on. I convey the feeling that it's fine, it's okay, I have no imperative and this makes them comfortable. It is merely the opportunity to have a conversation (personal interview with Andrew Urban, April 2000).

Concentration and listening

Well known Australian radio journalist Jon Faine believes there are three essentials for every interview: preparation, concentration and listening. Listening is often described as a neglected skill but its importance in interviewing cannot be overstated.

> The key to whether I make a good job or a bad job of the day's interviews is whether I'm concentrating . . . If you've got a question written down you tend to be thinking while

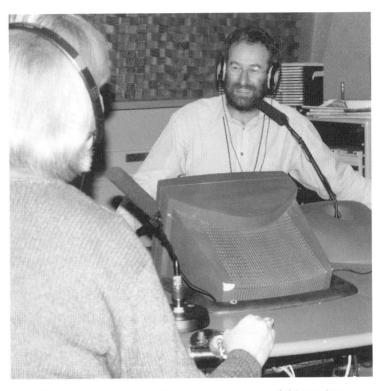

Jon Faine—listening is the key to every successful interview.
(Photo by Gail Sedorkin)

they're answering your second or third or fourth question, you're thinking, how am I going to phrase my next question. What's my segue into the next question, instead of actually listening to the bloody answer which will prob-ably give you the cue that you need for what is—in the audience's mind—the next most logical question to ask anyone. And if you stop listening to your guest's answers you'll miss things and you won't ask the most obvious thing which the audience are all shouting at you to ask as they're driving in the car, or in the kitchen doing the baking, and

The audience is following — you your logic should too.

15

they say 'how could you not ask that next question?'. The reason is because you weren't listening to the previous answer, because you were thinking about what you'd written down hours before sitting at your desk—and that's a very basic mistake (personal interview with Jon Faine, June 2000).

Silence

It is commonly agreed that silence can be a useful technique in interviewing. Sometimes used as an aggressive technique, journalists believe if they wait long enough the interviewee will feel obliged to fill up the space. However, this can be difficult for radio journalists who will be left with what is known as 'dead air'. In some interviews though, if the journalist wants 'considered' answers, they should be prepared to wait. Geraldine Doogue says with some interviewees you can 'hear the cogs whirring', and you should allow time for this process (ABC Radio, February 1999).

Respect and curiosity

Kerry O'Brien believes respect and curiosity are the most important 'natural assets' for interviewing. 'I think a respect for people is actually vital—curiosity about people, yes, but an understanding of a human being's basic right to a sense of dignity' (quoted in Wilson 2000:95). He believes curiosity is one of the fundamentals that drives journalism.

Let your curiosity flow. God knows where the expression curiosity killed the cat came from. Even when you're in a live situation and you're thinking 'I really want to ask this question but it's going to sound silly'. In most cases you should go ahead and ask it anyway. If it's a question that's driven by your natural curiosity, then there's every likelihood that other people would want to hear the answer too (personal interview with Kerry O'Brien, November 2000).

Andrew Urban believes the interview is like a small love affair. 'It's like falling in love a little bit at an intellectual level. And you know it happens when there is a sudden falling away of barriers, and they decide to trust you with their information' (personal interview with Andrew Urban, April 2000).

Andrew is well known for his ability to make people open up about their private lives—people he has never met before. How does he do it? He has three golden rules:

- Never judge people.
- Never make fun of people or manipulate them, never make a freak show.
- Always make them the centre of attention.

TECHNOLOGY

Technology has increased the number of ways that the interview is now conducted. Email and satellite interviews are used more frequently and are ideal tools for the journalist trying to contact people outside their time zone. While extremely useful for a journalist with limited time—and an interviewee with even less—these two interview forms have their drawbacks.

While most of the non-verbal clues are missed with a telephone interview, the tone of voice can be gauged and instant feedback helps prompt new questions. Email interviews lack spontaneity, allowing the interviewee time to consider and edit their answers with no direct pressure to answer the actual questions. Telephone and email interviews are covered in detail in Chapter 8. Satellite interviews have the advantage of allowing a 'real time' interview even when the two (or more) parties are not in the same city, state or country. However, not all satellite interviews have return vision (where both parties are able to see each other). The interviewee may be talking directly to a camera in another studio and may not be able to see the journalist—so again there may be a lack of non-verbal interaction.

Face-to-face interviews are preferable for journalists because they yield so much more information than the other methods. Not only are the answers articulated on the spot, but the body language of the interviewee can give clues for further questions and confirm the validity of the answers. Sometimes the non-verbal clues are more revealing than the verbal answers. It is a discouraging sign if a celebrity frowns after being asked about their private life. However, if they are leaning forward and smiling, it could be seen as a signal that they are happy to continue. Jon Faine says having the guest in the studio rather than interviewing on the telephone guarantees a better level of interaction between the guests and interviewer.

> It guarantees that the body language can come into play . . . You will always get your story told better if you agree to a studio interview, and some people insist on that. So we much prefer them, but it's just not physically possible within the constraints that many of our guests have on their working days, to come in and give us the time we would like to get from them (personal interview with Jon Faine, June 2000).

REFERENCES

Alysen, B. 2000, *The Electronic Reporter*, Deakin University Press, Geelong

Australian Broadcasting Corporation Radio 1999, 'Interview of the Week with Alan Saunders', Radio National, 5 February 1999

Bell, P. and van Leeuwen, T. 1994, *Media Interview—Confession, Contest, Conversation*, University of New South Wales Press, Sydney

Masterton, M. and Patching, R. 1997, *Now the News in Detail*, Deakin University Press, Geelong

Moore, B. (ed.) 1997, *The Australian Concise Oxford Dictionary of Current English*, 3rd edn, Oxford University Press, Melbourne

Personal interview with Peter Davis, June 2000

Personal interview with Clive Dorman, June 2000

Personal interview with Jon Faine, June 2000

Personal interview with Sharon Hill, November 2000

Personal interview with Al Morrison, August 2000

Personal interview with Kerry O'Brien, November 2000

Personal interview with Andrew Urban, April 2000

Wilson, R. 2000, *A Big Ask: Interviews with Interviewers*, New Holland Publishers, Sydney

http://www.abc.net.au/7.30/stories/s126909.html

http://www.bbc.co.uk/politics97/diana/panorama.html

http://www.pbs.org/wgbh/pages/frontline/shows/royals/interviews/bbc.html

2

RESEARCH

Nine out of ten of those who appear in 'The Rich List' don't want to talk about their money, says Graham Hunt, editor-at-large of *The National Business Review*. So how is the annual, bestselling list of New Zealand's rich and powerful compiled? 'Research, research, research' is Hunt's answer. 'We are able to read about dot.com magnates, about the sporting rich and about "old" money families because of old-fashioned journalistic digging. The research is undertaken by twelve staff reporters and researchers, an editor and a journalist brought in as a valuation expert. Without it "The Rich List" could not be published because very few people want to be interviewed about their wealth. This is just one example of the value of research in journalism, publishing a major feature when people <u>won't</u> talk to you' (personal interview with Graham Hunt, August 2000).

But in contexts other than financial investigations what use is research? Why should research be undertaken before an interview and what happens when you don't have enough time?

The national deputy news editor for Special Broadcasting Service (SBS) Radio, Sally Spalding, believes that if you don't do your research, then you're not doing your job properly.

> You have to do your research to do your job well, and to do justice to your job, and to do a good interview you're going to need that information. You can do an average job, or a mediocre job, but you won't get the best answers (personal interview with Sally Spalding, July 2001).

WHY RESEARCH?

[handwritten annotations: "this so that we can ask better questions. Notice how the chapter reads"]

Here are eight main reasons why research is useful.

1. Research helps you establish credibility as a reporter. It takes a certain amount of courage to ask questions, particularly if you have never met the interviewee before. Those you interview will be more inclined to talk to reporters who have done their homework and gathered background information. Leading British celebrity interviewer Lynn Barber talks about credibility and research:

   > I do begin an interview with a long, clever, scripted question which might go something like 'In 1968 you said in a *Times* interview that bla bla bla, whereas in 1988 you told the *Tatler* that bla bla bla. What happened between those dates to make you change your mind?' The object of this convoluted codswallop is simply to say, 'Look I've done a lot of homework for this interview. I have read all the cuttings; I expect you to make an effort now I am here' (Barber, 1991: xiv).

2. Research improves your confidence in asking 'hard' questions. Knowing that you have a document up your sleeve

or quotes or comments from someone else, or information from another source to reinforce the question you have asked, gives you the courage to press for answers. Tough or embarrassing questions often have to be asked, which may provoke a hostile reaction. Doing your homework means there is less chance of having your ignorance exposed.

3. Research enables you to get more out of an interviewee. For example, imagine interviewing New Zealand Prime Minister Helen Clark for a feature profile. A reporter has researched her love of mountain climbing, including her ascent of Mt Kilimanjaro in Africa. The journalist would be able to use this information in the interview either as an icebreaker or as a clever metaphor for the qualities needed to climb the greasy

Sally Spalding (right) *with Florence Houghton, 94, at the United Nations Association of Australia Media Peace Prize awards night, celebrating their win.* (Photograph by Peter Bennetts)

pole of politics. The Prime Minister is likely to be more expansive in this interview than if you are unprepared.

Sally Spalding of SBS says you can go in and try to wing it just by using the five 'w's and the one 'h', but often you need a lot more than that.

That's good for the basic start, but to do something on a deeper level, which is more an exposé of someone's personality, or character . . . you need to have a lot more information. So research in that sense is vital. And also you don't want to make a mistake . . . If you get your facts wrong you're going to look like a bit of an idiot because you don't really know what you're talking about. It looks like you're bluffing.

One example I have is: I interviewed this woman, who was 93 at the time, to do a radio piece on her. What happened was I found out a lot of information about her from the local priest, because she used to go to church on Sundays (even though when you met her she wouldn't have struck you as the church-going type!). It was really important to me to get as much information about her as I could so that when I went to do the interview I knew practically everything there was to know about her life.

So what happened was I had to condense down what probably was about 30 minutes of interview down to about 11 minutes for radio, and it's easy to lose the audience in 11 minutes so you have to keep it really dynamic and tight and really interesting. Because I knew so much of her life story and she had done so much as well, I was able to condense down all of those questions so that it was 11 minutes of dynamic radio. It resulted in me winning the United Nations Association of Australia Media Peace Prize for that year. That's one example where research was vital and led to a really positive result (personal interview with Sally Spalding, July 2001).

4. Research allows you to know when someone you are interviewing is avoiding the question, or evading the truth. Journalists and tax collectors have something in common: they learn to recognise the infinite ways interviewees can fudge facts in difficult situations. Fact fudging may be the result of acts of omission when information is withheld, acts of commission when lies are told, unintentional misleadings and deliberate red herrings. Increasingly, too, reporters covering areas such as politics or commerce have to pierce the shield of public relations practitioners who are guarding their clients. A recognition of the pitfalls and shortfalls of spin doctoring is possible if you have done your homework.

5. Research helps you understand trends, patterns and relationships. Some of the best stories written come from reporters who not only have an eye for spot news, but can see an 'issues' story developing. From their experience, from talking to sources, from reading, and from looking back over their clippings and listening back to their tapes and videos, they recognise social, political or economic trends. Whether your particular round is health, education, local politics or crime, you should be able to write or script topical backgrounders by keeping abreast of unfolding developments.

6. Research helps you keep an upbeat pace during an on-air or live broadcast interview. Kim Hill, Radio New Zealand's *Nine to Noon* interviewer, says, 'the more research you do, the faster on your feet you are. I think that's the main object of an interview, to be fast on your feet. Otherwise the interview gets bogged down, and you get stuck on one issue. You need to know enough about a subject to

volley . . . (quoted with permission from Kim Hill from *Advanced Interviewing Skills for Journalists*, National Diploma in Journalism, 1996).

7. Research allows you to angle the news so you are not repeating stories others have already broadcast or written. Chief reporters and news editors would doubtless cite as their greatest frustration the number of stories presented to them by reporters that do not freshen up a running story with a new angle.

8. Research improves accuracy. It helps untangle incorrect information and verify facts, dates, names, numbers and what sources have said previously. Remember, you owe it to the people you interview to get it right. It has been said that the interview is a conversation with consequences. The celebrities, the politicians, the officials, the sports people, the eye witnesses and the ordinary people in the street who are interviewed by journalists are being judged not just by the reporter but by everyone who reads, watches, or hears their comments.

THE TIME FACTOR

Time is the enemy of good reporting. All reporters feel that in some interviews they haven't asked the right question or gained the most from a newsworthy person because their preparation time for the interview was limited. So what can you do when you have no time for detailed research? The pace of the newsroom means that few reporters have the luxury of research for every interview. They often hurtle to airports or meetings armed only with native cunning, a scrappy assignment note and tape recorder, camera crew or a notepad.

Political interviewer Kerry O'Brien says there will be many situations where you're handed an assignment and you've got to rush out the door.

But in this day of mobile phones you just might be able to—if you're working with an organisation that has the resources of a library—check on clippings while you're on the run. Maybe there's someone knowledgeable that you can think of that you can phone as you're on your way to an interview, to try and flesh something out for you (personal interview with Kerry O'Brien, November 2000).

Here are two research strategies—one short-term and one long-term—for discovering background information when you know little or nothing about the person who you will be interviewing.

Short-term strategy: Ask naively dumb, but not completely stupid, questions

Most people you interview realise that journalists cannot be experts on every subject and every person. There are times when you have to be brave enough to ask naively dumb questions without appearing completely stupid. Coax the subject of the interview to explain the background of a conflict, dispute or issue so that your readers, listeners or viewers will understand. Asking technical experts to explain something complex in lay terms is another way of getting the story without revealing your ignorance. Another technique is to encourage eye witnesses to tell their story in their own words first so you can pick up enough to ask relevant follow-on questions. Never pretend to know more than you do. The humble journalist who flatters the interviewee and coaxes answers from them will come away with a better story than the reporter who feigns knowledge and writes in ignorance. Be honest enough to say you don't understand or don't know when it is appropriate so that interviewees provide the missing information.

Long-term strategy: Develop background knowledge to rely on

Curiosity killed the cat—but it sustains the journalist. Journalists are by nature, and by calling, inquisitive. To be professionally curious, though, reporters need to build their own banks of knowledge about the rounds they cover, their communities, politics and the issues of the day. The more information you store about a topic, the more curious you become about the unanswered questions and the unexplained doubts. This background knowledge can be the journalist's secret weapon and it can form the basis of interview questions when you have had no direct time to research a specific interviewee.

Background knowledge is developed by:

- your own personal reading
- seeking out news and current affairs through watching television, listening to the radio and reading newspapers and magazines
- regular contact with your sources
- talking to other journalists in the newsroom, particularly the good reporters
- involving the librarian in your job so she or he alerts you to anything you might not see or hear
- thinking about your work

When you have no time for formal research you will be more confident about asking the spontaneous question because you have invested in your own bank of background knowledge and current affairs information.

Sally Spalding of SBS Radio advocates the long-term strategy of developing background knowledge.

You have to make sure that you're on top of the topic by listening to the radio each day in the morning to the top stories . . . You should also try to see at least one TV bulletin each night . . . The best journalists that we've ever hired into our level one position (which is our entry level position) . . . are the ones that always come in the door in the morning for an eight o'clock start and have read the papers at home before they get to work. They're the most impressive staff that we've had. And the ones that get to work and think 'I'll read the papers when I get there', never hit the ground with their feet running, because you have to brief them before they go out on a story. Well my expectation is that they know the story before they get here, not that we have to tell them what they should be asking and what the story's about (personal interview with Sally Spalding, July 2001).

FINDING THE ANGLE

One news editor used visual aids to teach young reporters the value of an 'angle'. He would make the first folio of the hard copy of the story that was not up to standard into a paper dart. That was before he spiked it. This taught journalists in the newsroom to spend extra time finding an angle.

New Zealand journalist Deborah Telford (1999), writing about interviewing for new reporters, suggests you find out what your editor/chief reporter or the news desk wants from the story. What angle is required and what length should the story be? Is the story merely a reaction piece to splice into a longer story, or is it a full interview?

SBS's Sally Spalding says research is essential to find the angle that no-one else has got.

That's the story we're always looking for. We never want the mainstream angle because we can always get that off the wires anyway. We're always looking for the other angle that's of relevance to SBS—and that only comes from research and having that background knowledge (personal interview with Sally Spalding, July 2001).

For example, the newsroom may have received an anonymous tip-off and wants you to put the information to someone, or radio may want follow-up reaction to a story that appeared in the first edition of the morning paper.

But remember, don't just blindly follow newsroom advice. Act on your hunches too, and don't close your mind to new surprise angles in a story.

Before beginning the research ask yourself:

• How much do I know about the subject?
• What do I want to find out (the litmus test for this might be to ask yourself what is it that the public wants to know)?
• Where can I find the information?
• What is the quickest way to retrieve it?

CLIPPINGS BOOKS AND COMPUTER FILES

Clippings books provide a speedy update on stories. The time-honoured tradition of cutting and pasting the stories you write for print media into scrapbooks is alive and well in most newsrooms. Veteran New Zealand prize-winning environmental reporter John Saunders said, 'you've always got to know where the story has got to' (personal interview with John Saunders, August 2000). Referring to clippings books as a living resource means you do not repeat old news or begin at the wrong start point. He recalls an embarrassing newsroom episode when a novice reporter who conducted no research and had no access to a clippings book fell for a story from a man interviewed at the front counter who suggested that the historic, disused bridge over the Manawatu River should be dismantled for safety reasons. The story was front-paged in the *Evening Standard* even though the regular city council reporter had written it several times previously. Clippings books become part of your CV and can be used to show off your stories when applying for other newsroom jobs. Electronic filing is useful and now major news outlets have their own search engines that provide electronic updates.

LIBRARIES

The best advice for a new reporter in the newsroom or at university is to immediately make friends with the librarian. Librarians are secret resources. They know where to get information and how to get information. They can save you from mistakes and alert you to story possibilities. In newsrooms where the reporter population is young and mobile, it is often the librarian who has the most historical knowledge of events and issues in the area. In some newsrooms the librarian attends daily news conferences and is given the assignment list to begin collecting information for the interviews of the day. Where there is no newsroom librarian, public library facilities offer similar but often less specific resources.

TIP:

Make a friend of your librarian—they can help make or break good interviews

---

Most media libraries have moved to electronic access, although in some newspaper libraries there is currently a combination of clippings back in history and contemporary electronic filing. Past happenings, and even people, can be accessed via photographic negative searches.

You may be located close to specialist libraries such as technical libraries, archives and university libraries. Whatever story you are researching there is likely to be a matching specialist library that general librarians can help you find.

'LIVING TREASURES'

In every community there are people with astonishing knowledge about issues and events. Finding these 'living treasures' and exploiting their reservoirs of knowledge is an art form. Some reporters have very good contacts because they 'work their sources'. For example, your news editor tells you on Monday morning that you are to write a feature story on the rising tide of youth crime for Saturday's feature section. Make a note of where you would start and whom you would speak to. Sources could include the local police chief, victims support group, school teachers and principals, parents, young people themselves, youth aid workers, community groups and lawyers, politicians and perhaps criminologists or academics interested in youth crime. During the process of interviewing these sources you will find one or two people significantly more resourceful than others. They will make good copy. They will point you in other directions for information and source material, open doors and provide access for you. Make sure you keep their contact details and telephone these 'living treasures' regularly for news tips. These key informants are the lifeblood of journalism.

RESEARCHERS

Some elite interviewers have the services of a full-time researcher. When Dr Brian Edwards hosted the popular Saturday morning radio program *Top O' the Morning* on New Zealand's National Radio, the interviews he conducted had been meticulously planned and prepared by a full-time researcher. He placed such a premium on research that he personally paid the salary of the researcher from his fee for the program. The researcher would conduct full-length interviews with subjects and pass information on to Brian, who then conducted his own interview that went to air.

'INTERVIEWING' VIA THE COMPUTER

'They are raising the ante on what it takes to be a journalist' was the way American author Philip Meyer opened his book, *The New Precision Journalism*. Meyer was referring to the new methods in computer-assisted research and reporting (CARR). Computer-assisted reporting will be in every reporter's job description in the near future.

Soon no paper files will exist, predicts American media commentator Cecilia Friend. Reporters seeking local information at a local council or courtroom will not be able to poke into a paper file. Instead they will have to 'interview' computers for information previously gained from paper files.

There are two major forms of computer-assisted reporting.
1. Retrieving background information and data from online computer access. This is a reconfiguration of the traditional research function using paper files or asking questions of sources.
2. Computer-assisted data analysis that allows journalists to 'interview' computers and provides a neutral approach to

raw information. You can avoid relying on both the word of others and on supplied statistics already interpreted for you.

Warning

While computer-assisted research and reporting is an exciting prospect, sole reliance on information from a computer can be risky. New Zealand's *National Business Review* editor-at-large, Graham Hunt, says 'the computer can never be a real substitute for primary documents. Recently we were doing a story about a crooked property developer. While we had computer access to credit checks . . . we are always conscious that people can have the same or similar names, and that relatively unskilled people can enter data. If we're doing a hard-hitting story then to be safe we need an audit trail of primary records' (personal interview with Graham Hunt, August 2000).

Journalism sites focusing on new media

Billed as 'everything you need to be a better journalist', the Poynter Institute offers many great resources for journalists all on one site at <http://www.poynter.org>. If you become interested in computer-assisted reporting, one not-to-be-missed site is the National Institute of Computer-Assisted Reporting at <http://www.nicar.org>. An allied site is the Investigative Reporters and Editors' site at <www.ire.org>. These are American Websites, but contain a wealth of ideas and information that is useful to all practitioners.

Need to find a specialist source? One place to start is ProfNet <http://www.profnet.com>. It links journalists to academics in the United States, United Kingdom and Germany. Send an email request or search the site's database of experts. (ProfNet is owned by PR Newswire.)

Finding information fast

The University of Queensland's Belinda Weaver has developed one of the best sources of online information and contacts for journalists in Australia, Ozguide. This page was created (in a personal capacity) by Belinda, the Library Liaison for Journalism, Social Sciences and Humanities Library, and it is located at: <http://www.sjc.uq.edu.au/ozguide/index.html>.

It covers everything from government (including *Hansard*) and non-government organisations to phone directories, all accessed from a 'rounds'-based structure, which then links to numerous other sites and home pages. When you go to this address you will find two other outstanding sites developed by Belinda—Foreign Correspondent and Globalisation.

For an excellent book on searching the World Wide Web, please see Virginia Earle's *Searching the Web: A Smart Guide to On-line Skills* (1999). Personal favourites, from the many Virginia mentions in her book, include Anzwers, a search engine that is trustworthy and offers a drop-down search menu. Find Anzwers at <http://www.anzwers.co.nz>.

Another comprehensive book on searching the World Wide Web is Stephen Quinn's *Newsgathering on the Net* (2001). This is a recently released second edition so includes up-to-date tips and sites.

Please note: other useful sites are included in Appendix A, but remember Websites come and go.

RESEARCHING FOR INVESTIGATIVE JOURNALISM

In his book, *Deadline*, renowned New Zealand investigative journalist Pat Booth dispels the myth that investigative journalism is glamorous. It is 'tough, long, hard and sometimes expensive' and sometimes does not have the wholehearted support of management, even though your editor may support you. Booth's seven-year investigation into the Arthur Allan Thomas case (a famous double murder trial which eventually saw Thomas freed from gaol and pardoned) was done in his own time. He says, 'Three times I deliberately ignored top-level instructions to let the issue drop' (1997: 214).

Investigative journalists like Pat Booth make personal sacrifices to dig deep. Their investigative research comprises hundreds of interviews with different people over a long time. An excellent book to prepare yourself for researching for investigative journalism is Amanda Cropp's *Digging Deeper* (1997) published by the New Zealand Journalists Training Organisation.

REFERENCES

Barber, L. 1991, *Mostly Men*, Viking, London

Booth, P. 1997, *Deadline*, Penguin Books, Auckland

Cropp, A. 1997, *Digging Deeper: A New Zealand Guide to Investigative Reporting*, New Zealand Journalists Training Organisation, Wellington

Earle, V. 1999, *Searching the Web: A Smart Guide to On-line Skills*, The Open Polytechnic of New Zealand, Lower Hutt, New Zealand

Friend, C. 1994, 'Daily newspaper use of computers to analyze data', in *Newspaper Research Journal*, vol. 15, No. 1. Winter, pp. 63-72

Hill, K. 1996, *Advanced Interviewing Skills for Journalists*, National Diploma in Journalism, Wellington Polytechnic and the Open Polytechnic of New Zealand, Wellington

Meyer, P. 1991, *The New Precision Journalism*, Indiana University Press, Bloomington, Indiana

Personal interview with Graham Hunt, August 2000

Personal interview with Kerry O'Brien, November 2000

Personal interview with John Saunders, August 2000

Personal interview with Sally Spalding, July 2001

Quinn, S. 2001, 2nd edition *Newsgathering on the Net*, Macmillan, South Yarra

Telford, D. 1999, 'Interviewing', in *A Beginner's Guide to Professional News Journalism*, ed. J. Tucker, New Zealand Journalists Training Organisation, pp. 81-5

http://www.anzwers.co.nz

http://www.ire.org

http://www.nicar.org

http://www.poynter.org

http://www.profnet.com

http://www.sjc.uq.edu.au/ozguide/index.html

3
GETTING STARTED

Former New Zealand Prime Minister Sir Robert Muldoon struck terror into usually cocky journalists. He banned several senior journalists from Parliament, he refused to talk to a leading Sunday newspaper for two years, and he always taped his own interviews so he could complain later. Author and journalist Peter Hawes wrote about his television interview with 'Piggy' Muldoon. Muldoon demonstrated a 'menace which literally brought your belly very close to your bowels. To interview Muldoon you needed to memorise some questions so in the event of acute mental paralysis you could switch to a sort of automatic parrot and at least blurt out something' (1996: 157).

PSYCHING YOURSELF UP FOR THE INTERVIEW

Not all interviewees are as formidable as Muldoon was. Psyching yourself up for an interview is only one of several techniques and behaviours necessary for getting started as an interviewer. The more preparation you have undertaken for an interview the more relaxed and efficient you are likely to be. Remember, it is not just new journalists who become nervous before interviews. Even journalists who have conducted hundreds of interviews have their adrenaline pumping as they ask that first question.

Telephone terror or phone phobia is not uncommon and can paralyse reporters who have to ring people they do not know, or when they have to ask 'hard' questions. It is often the inevitability of a creeping deadline and a pushy chief reporter or news editor that forces you to pick up the phone. Death-knock interviews, confrontational interviews where reporters have to challenge people about what they have said and interviewing witnesses after tragedies all demand courage.

TIP: TO HELP THE PSYCHING-UP PROCESS

1. Take a few deep breaths.
2. Rehearse your opening lines to build confidence.

Then, just do it!

THE CONTACT BOOK

One tried and tested aid for getting started as an interviewer is the old faithful—the journalist's contact book. A veteran journalist once offered to sell his contact book to a colleague for $5000. The contact book had such a high value because the journalist religiously sought out and entered the after-hours numbers, mobile phone numbers and holiday address numbers of every single source he ever came in contact with. This scruffy address book, that had to be kept bound with rubber bands, was locked in the reporter's desk when he was out of the newsroom. A good contact book can mean the difference between getting an interview in time for deadline and failing to speak to someone who is hot news. Palm Pilots and other electronic files on computers can be useful too.

Start now

Start your contact book as soon as you start your first story— whether this is at university, a journalism training course or in the workplace. As soon as you make contact with a source, enter their details in your book. Don't put this task off. You may lose the information and then have to go through the same tedious methods of finding the source the next time you want an interview. Most journalists consider their contact book their 'bible' and would be lost without it. It is wise to keep a duplicate copy at home. Make sure your contact book is easy to carry around. To help with future research some journalists write the dates of stories beside the source's name in their book. One way to develop your contact book after an interview is to ask your source for any other people who should be contacted for the story. Don't forget to include email addresses for your contacts.

TIP:

Use a rating system where you put stars against the names of those contacts who supply accurate and timely information to you regularly. The more stars— the better the contact.

TOOLS OF THE TRADE ... RECORDERS AND NOTEPADS

As any reporter who has survived a libel action can testify, journalistic reputation rests on the quality of evidence that can be produced to prove that the interviewee said what was reported. Quality shorthand notes in a notepad and a recording are both good libel insurance. They provide evidence that you didn't misquote the source in an interview or that you didn't 'doctor' quotes. Each form of recording interviews has its advantages and drawbacks. In some newsrooms there is a prescribed protocol for data collection. In others it is up to the individual reporter. In either case the best advice is: be systematic.

Notepads and recordings (tapes/discs) should be as neatly annotated as possible with the interviewee's name, time and date of interview. After use they should be stored, not lost. If someone disputes an aspect of your story the last thing you want is a frantic hunt through the newsroom, flat or the office car to find your reporter's notepad. It pays to put a unique identifier with a marker pen on the front of your current notepad so no one else will pick it up by mistake.

TIP:

Develop a housekeeping system for your interview data. This will provide insurance against trouble, such as claims of misreporting or libel actions. Most newsrooms and news organisations insist that reporters keep interview data for a certain period before it is destroyed.

Recorders

A tape recorder or mini-disc recorder can make some people nervous and self-conscious and inhibit good quotes. But recording an interview does allow the reporter to maintain eye contact with the subject of the interview and that is valuable for picking up important non-verbal cues. Recording an interview also means that you concentrate on asking the 'right' questions, including succinct follow-up questions, rather than worrying about converting words to shorthand. Tapes and discs can be time-consuming to transcribe when working to daily print media deadlines but essential to provide voice for radio. Write your story first, then fast-forward through the tape or disc to find the quotes you require. During the interview, take enough notes to make it possible to write the story without the recording, in case the tape fails, and also to give an indication where material will appear on the tape or disc.

Whatever you take to record the interview, make sure it works; that your recording device has batteries and is correctly maintained; the machine is on 'record' when the interview starts; and that the microphone is placed so it can clearly pick up all that is said. Start the device before the interview by recording an 'ident' or identification: the time, the date, the name of the interviewee and your name. Ensuring you have quality audio for radio is essential.

TIP:

Don't use the 'voice activated' function of a recorder, as you tend to lose the first few words as the record function starts up.

Some journalists don't record their interviews because they believe they don't listen as intently, knowing they have the recording to fall back on. They feel this lack of concentrated attention means they might miss clues to future questions or angles. Others believe that recordings provide valuable insurance against accusations of bad reporting. Recorders can also break down so ensure you take sufficient notes, or you may return empty handed. Recorders are banned from parliaments, courts and most tribunals, so it is vital for reporters to learn shorthand.

Notepads

Shorthand is a cost effective and relatively fail-safe method of collecting interview data. Many reporters possess idiosyncratic, if not eccentric, shorthand—a blend of shorthand and longhand, abbreviated words and symbols. The average person speaks at approximately 160 words per minute while your shorthand expertise might only be 90 words per minute.

TIP:

When you are taking notes your news radar will tell you when you have been given a good quote or angle. Develop a system where you underline or put a star beside the best information as you take it down. This saves a lot of time when searching through your notes later.

BEFORE YOU START

In general an interview should provide the reader, listener or viewer with enough information to answer the proverbial five

Ws and one H: Who, What, When, Where, Why and How. The interview should: establish *relevance* (for example, Hollywood movie actor Russell Crowe is home visiting family and promoting his latest movie); be *timely* (conducted either before or during his visit); and capture *interest* (seductive introduction, great 'grab' and sparkling quotes).

Each interview will have its own unique rationale but some generic lines of inquiry include life and death, motivations, aspirations, past achievements, future challenges, current projects, future prospects, state of humanity, social problems, business and industry concerns, political conflict and personal circumstances. Many great interviews arise from the tension between previous statements and current actions.

TIP:

Don't forget that interviews are essentially about what interests us most—people.

Before you get started you need to answer two questions about the interview.
— What info do you need?

1. What is the point of the interview? You should have the purpose clear in your mind. A lack of focus is one of the main causes of poor interviews. British celebrity interviewer Lynn Barber suggests there is a behavioural problem about interviewing for some beginner journalists, 'simply because they're confused about what they're doing. They want to be liked, they want to make an impression and find common ground with the interviewee. Which means they want the interview to be a conversation, a dialogue, the

start of a beautiful friendship' (1999: xiii). Barber states journalists must remember that they are there on behalf of the readers. Highly respected Australian political journalist Laurie Oakes agrees: 'I don't think an interview can ever be like a conversation. Conversations are, by definition, unstructured. If you go to an interview without having some idea of where it's going and what you want out of it, it's hopeless. I think you need to plan an interview, to have a purpose when you start out' (quoted in Wilson 2000: 104).

2. Who should you interview to gather the information? Very often the right person is obvious, you know the source and that they have the information. At other times the question of whom to approach won't be so obvious. In these cases it is better to start with the management of the organisation, for example, and be directed to the right person.

In reporting on cultures or religions other than ones you are familiar with, you may be unclear about whom to approach for comment. In New Zealand, for example, if you are a New Zealand European, or Pakeha, it can be difficult to know whom to approach for comment on Maori issues. Maori have a word, *mangainui*, for big mouths who are always ready to comment on anything even though they have no authority. In Australia, it is important to know the tribal name and the region of the tribe, and particularly not to refer to Torres Strait Islanders or Aborigines as one and the same, as they are two distinct peoples. The protocol on Aboriginal communities requires that journalists approach the tribal Elders first before interviewing other members of the community. If this system is not followed it can have major repercussions for the journalist, as well as the members of the community who spoke to the journalist.

or peg

THE NEWS ANGLE

Before you start writing up an interview or going to air you need to decide on the angle for the story. Often the angle hits you instantly, and sometimes there is a wealth of possible introductions. At other times you sit staring at the blank computer screen or repeatedly replay your interview in the hope that inspiration arrives.

Writing a great news angle is one of the joys and one of the mysteries of journalism. In Rene J. Cappon's great little book on good news writing, *The Word*, the news angle is described as 'the agony of square one' (1982: 31). It's easy to identify what isn't a great news angle. These include stories that start with areas which have been examined thoroughly in previous interviews, stories that mumble and stumble their way forward, stories that don't grab readers, and stories whose introductions are cluttered with secondary detail, chronology and abstraction.

TIP: TO IDENTIFY A NEWS ANGLE ASK YOURSELF:

- What's different or new about the information?
- What details distinguish this story from others of its kind?
- What will 'grab' the attention of readers, listeners or viewers?

The real key to lifting your head out of the humdrum is to ask yourself what, about the particular story, is *different*. Much of the news is repetitive: war, crime, disaster. The goal, both in the lead and in the rest of the story, is to stress those angles that are least like the routine of other stories in this class. Many times this special element is there and writers overlook it. By overlooking it, they deprive themselves of the chance to equip their lead with that small hook that engages the reader's interest (Cappon 1982: 35).

In an interview keep thinking what questions you could ask to support your angle. Lynn Barber (1991) says the best interviews should sing the strangeness and variety of the human race. What questions will elicit this strangeness and variety? Because journalism is a competitive business you will often be operating against reporters from rival organisations. What will make *your* interview with a visiting celebrity, for example, different from the rest of the media? Your aim is to walk away with extra information the other journalists didn't get. A tip here is to hold back an original question and ask it after the formal media conference has ended when other journalists can't use the answer.

Remember, sometimes the news editor or chief reporter wants a particular 'angle' out of an interview because your report will be part of a story, or reaction to other comment. They need the information as quickly as possible and it is your first responsibility to get back to the newsroom with the information speedily. But never close your mind to an unexpected different snippet of information that reveals a new facet to the story.

WRITING QUESTIONS AND KEYWORDS

Journalists are almost equally divided over whether having a prepared list of questions is a good idea or not. Lynn Barber (1991) says she always prepares a list of written questions but it is only a prop. Some journalists believe that with a formal list of questions you risk limiting your news antennae to the assumptions expressed in the written questions. There is also a risk that you will not follow up on newsworthy answers with further prompts because you are slavishly tied to the questions on the prepared list. They argue that with a list you risk destroying the flow of an interview because the interviewer will not move away from the prepared, but predictable, questions towards what might be special and different that is signalled in the interviewee's previous answers. Others, particularly reporters who conduct profile, personality or extended interviews, suggest it is unprofessional not to have prepared questions, even if they are not all used during the interview. Journalists with less experience are advised to develop lists of questions. They help boost confidence, the process of devising them encourages good research habits and prepared questions do focus the interview.

There are two parts to preparing a question line.
1. Work out the general topic areas you want to cover, and
2. Prepare specific questions.

Keywords or catch phrases can be developed to remind you of general topic areas. For example, before an interview with visiting British journalist John Pilger, the following series of keywords and phrases would help keep general topic areas in mind:

- Role of journalist–activist v. reflector
- State of news generally
- International response to investigative journalism
- Personal safety in dangerous locations
- Controversy over the Pilger style
- Current projects
- Future projects

- Past, present and future—East Timor, Cambodia, Vietnam and race relations in Australia.

Whether you have a set of keywords or a prepared list of questions you need to be thinking ahead as the interview unfolds. In Colin Dexter's crime novels his famous characters, the intelligent and intuitive Inspector Morse and the method-ical Sergeant Lewis, have very different styles of detective work. Journalism and detective work have qualities in common. The brilliant Inspector Morse possesses a quality that Sergeant Lewis admires and is found in many top reporters. It is the:

> . . . knack of *prospective thinking*, of looking ahead and asking oneself the right questions, as well as the wrong questions, about what was likely to happen in the future; and then of coming up with some answers, be they right or wrong (1999: 138).

ORGANISING YOURSELF

Organising yourself before the interview is another important aspect of getting started. Here are four organisational tips.

1. Dress appropriately for the interview context. If you are interviewing political or business leaders a suit and tie or sports jacket for men and business clothes for women should be worn. Other contexts may require different dress styles. For example, female reporters covering a Maori tangi funeral should dress in black and wear a long skirt if possible to acknowledge Maori custom at a funeral. A female reporter once gained an exclusive interview during

the Mr Asia drug case with notorious New Zealand criminal Peter Fulcher at his heavily secured North Shore house. She had to go alone and wore jeans and running shoes for convenience and a quick escape if necessary.

2. Have maps, addresses, telephone contacts and all the destination details with you when setting out on an interview assignment. Don't rely on photographers or other members of the camera crew to know where you should be going.

3. Let the newsroom know where you are at all times, and alert them to whether or not you have the story as the deadline looms, or that the angle of the story may have changed. Your information or quotes from an interview may be vital for the front page lead or the hourly bulletin and can be read back over a mobile phone.

4. Be aware that you might have to go out quickly to interview disaster victims, witnesses to an emergency, or to a spot news event. Develop an 'on call' persona so that the chief reporter or news editor chooses you for the unexpected and interesting interview assignments. This state of suspended adrenaline is half the fun of being a reporter.

TIP:

As a general rule, don't supply questions in advance to people you are about to interview. If you do, you risk losing the element of surprise essential in many media interviews and it can allow interviewees to manage and 'spin' their responses. It can also inhibit spontaneity when you are seeking colourful quotes.

ACCESSING THE INTERVIEW

Gaining access to the person you want to interview can be as simple as calling a telephone number. It can also be a major challenge.

Making appointments

For many routine stories reporters can make a timely appointment on the day with a local official, business person or police chief for an interview to gather information for a story. Punctuality, courtesy and keeping faith by turning up, and conducting an interview efficiently to minimise time inconvenience to the interviewee become second nature to reporters writing routine news stories. But what happens when you can't get past a gatekeeper, an overly protective secretary, or an officious minder?

Dropping in unannounced

Using surprise tactics is a familiar journalistic technique for getting to people who don't want to talk to you. Going to someone's office and asking for comment, waiting in a carpark beside a car, staking out an airport entrance or the side door of a courtroom, are regular practices for reporters, photographers and camera crews. There is no universally successful formula for getting someone who doesn't want to speak or comment, even though gathering all sides of a story is enshrined as a fundamental principle of journalistic fairness. There is a measure of luck involved in gaining access to a reluctant interviewee. But it is far more likely that persistence rather than luck wins the story.

TIPS: TO GET PAST THE GATEKEEPERS

- Be persistent and don't give up.
- If the gatekeeper won't put you through on the telephone after the first and second attempts, then try and get a letter, facsimile or email to the person who is being protected. In some cases the potential source of the news really doesn't mind talking to reporters and the gatekeeper simply assumes the role of keeping you out.
- In exceptional cases it may be appropriate to drop off a list of written questions that would form the basis of the interview. Then, if the source still will not comment, the questions can be referred to in the story with the phrase that 'such and such was unavailable for comment'.
- If it is appropriate (check with your chief reporter or news editor) the gatekeeper should be told politely but firmly that it is in the public interest that the information be sought and that stone-walling is unacceptable.
- Always try to find the mobile phone numbers of potential sources of news. These are numbers they usually answer themselves. You may find yourself straight through to the Prime Minister, the bikie gang leader, the shy sports star or the elusive celebrity.
- Remember ministerial press secretaries paid by the public purse are *expected* to provide access and act as a link between Cabinet ministers and the media. You are entitled to remind them of their obligations if they are overly protective and try to shut you out.

THE GOOD, THE BAD AND THE UGLY: DEALING WITH PUBLIC RELATIONS PRACTITIONERS

The higher the stakes in politics, professional sport and corporate business the more likely there is to be a professional media minder 'guarding' the sources of news. Journalists need to learn how to deal with PR people and combat their strategies if they are to get stories.

The good

In her guide to investigative reporting New Zealand's Amanda Cropp says that 'if you need accurate background facts fast PR people can be enormously helpful and they understand the drawbacks of saying "no comment" ' (1997: 20). In instances such as civil defence emergencies where the public relations spokesperson is the conduit for information, or police media relations officers handling spot crime news, a strong relationship of trust and reciprocity can develop between journalists and PR people. The majority of public relations practitioners see their job altruistically as a positive influence between clients as sources of the news and the news media. In some cases such as the police, fire service or other emergency services the public relations spokesperson is trained in the service they represent and simply want to present it in the best possible light.

TIP: USE PR PEOPLE TO:

- Provide background information
- Arrange access for the interview
- Indicate where sources can be found for comment
- Provide one perspective on the news

The bad

Tension will always exist between journalists and PR people simply because PR is a barrier between reporters and direct sources of the news. Who wants to interview a celebrity minder, or a politician's 'spin doctor'? The public expects the real thing. Despite the rapid growth of the news management business, the public, too, retains a healthy scepticism about PR. Rodney Tiffen, in his book about the news media and Australian politics, notes 'the most heartening feature of public relations politics is how often it fails' (1985: 85). While PR people can be helpful, New Zealand's Karl du Fresne, writing in *Free Press Free Society*, says of PR people:

> Their employers expect them to orchestrate news releases to best advantage, to disguise or play down potentially embarrassing information and to deflect or defuse damaging inquiries. Sometimes they exert pressure on editors to restrain reporters whose stories are making life uncomfortable. They also give advice and training to corporate executives on how to 'handle' the media—which often means evading difficult questions (1995: 40).

TIP: DO NOT ALLOW PR PEOPLE TO:

- Dictate the terms and conditions of an interview
- Spin the angles in your news story
- Deny you legitimate access to an interviewee

And the ugly

Two American researchers, James Tankard and Randy Sumpter (1993), make the worrying claim that journalists are becoming more and more accepting of 'spin doctors'. They maintain that this is disturbing when you think about what 'spin doctors' do, which is to try to manipulate the slant, angle or frame that will be used in news reports. That should be the job of the journalist and not a source with a vested interest. It is clear, too, that in a number of areas, particularly politics, sport, big business and former government agencies that have been corporatised, such as health boards in New Zealand and Telstra in Australia, there is a growing imbalance in resources between newsrooms and the PR machine. Good journalists constantly fight to maintain the independence and autonomy of their news. So always ask yourself:

- What's the spin here?
- Have I too freely accepted the PR version?
- Have I spoken to a range of other sources?
- Will an interview with someone else provide a truer picture?

TIPS:

1. Always try for your own interview with a source named in a supplied press release. This is superior to a simple rewrite of someone else's work, and allows you to double-check the contents. It also means you are not hostage to the 'spin'.

2. Consult other reporters and the codes of ethics that apply to you before accepting benefits, favours and 'perks' from PR people. Gifts, liquor, travel and tickets to shows and sporting events may not appear to be a problem until a favour is expected of you in return.

REFERENCES

Barber, L. 1991, *Mostly Men*, Viking, London

—— 1999, *The Demon Barber*, Penguin, London

Cappon, R.J. 1982, *The Word: An Associated Press Guide to Good News Writing*, The Associated Press, New York

Cropp, A. 1997, *Digging Deeper: A New Zealand Guide to Investigative Reporting*, New Zealand Journalists Training Organisation, Wellington

Dexter, C. 1999, *The Remorseful Day*, MacMillan, London

du Fresne, K. 1995, *Free Press Free Society*, Newspaper Publishers Association, Wellington

Hawes, P. 1996, 'Memoirs of a spear carrier: the political television interviews of Peter Hawes', in *Dangerous Democracy? News Media Politics in New Zealand*, ed. J. McGregor, Dunmore Press, Palmerston North, pp. 149–55

Tankard, J.W. & Sumpter, R. 1993, 'Media awareness of media manipulation: the use of the term "spin doctor"', Paper presented to the Mass Communication and Society Division of the Association for Education in Journalism and Mass Communication, Kansas City, Missouri

Tiffen, R. 1985, *News and Power*, Allen & Unwin, Sydney

Wilson, R. 2000, *A Big Ask: Interviews with Interviewers*, New Holland Publishers, Sydney

4

BREAKING THE ICE

Anyone who conducts interviews regularly will undoubtedly tell you the first few minutes of the interview are the most crucial. This is the 'first impressions' time that can make or break an interview. It's this informal time before an interview that sets the atmosphere and the tone, and the time to establish a rapport with the interviewee. These first few minutes are critical and can be the key to a great interview—or, in some cases, getting an interview at all. A common technique to get the conversation rolling is known as an icebreaker. It can take anywhere from ten seconds to ten minutes, sometimes longer, but is an essential start to any interview. Icebreakers can be divided into two main categories:

1. Research icebreakers, and
2. On-the-spot icebreakers.

Research icebreakers are devised as a result of the journalist's knowledge of, and research on, the interviewee. These icebreakers are preferable and are one preparation technique that is practically guaranteed to produce positive results. If it is a spontaneous event, which does not allow the luxury of time for research, the interviewer must then rely on their observation skills or general knowledge to formulate an 'on-the-spot' icebreaker.

Australian journalist Peter Davis recalls using a joke as an icebreaker when he was interviewing a reluctant Queen's Counsel.

> He would only do the interview at his chambers, which immediately put me at a disadvantage. In the studio I'm comfortable—but I definitely wasn't in his imposing chambers. As soon as I sat down he said: 'I won't talk about my law firm and I won't talk about my family'. So my first question was: 'How much money does your firm bring in each week and how many illegitimate children do you have?' It certainly broke the ice! (personal interview with Peter Davis, June 2000).

BEFORE THE ICEBREAKER   *Remember our mantra.*

Before you get to use your icebreaker, your initial contact with the interviewee should be polite but confident. Shake hands firmly (without crushing bones), introduce yourself and greet your interviewee. Australian political journalist Kerry O'Brien believes it's a straightforward courtesy to shake a person's hand when you meet them for the first time, or if you're welcoming somebody into your studio or into your domain. 'I think it's only sensible unless you're dealing with an axe murderer who's just been recaptured.'

> There's an onus on you to offer basic courtesies of politeness. I think it's in your interest for a better outcome if you can make that person feel comfortable. But you don't have

to be obsequious, in fact I would hope that you wouldn't be. And you don't have to be too deferential. A straightforward handshake is enough, then if it's the Prime Minister, you might say 'thank you for coming in to the studio Prime Minister'. I think you can apply that equally to most people in most situations unless they've signalled to you that they wanted you to call them by their first name. If it's somebody who is so familiar—like Tiger Woods—you'd feel a little bit silly saying Mr Woods when the world calls him Tiger. Use your instincts in that regard (personal interview with Kerry O'Brien, November 2000).

WHEN?

The time for your icebreaker is before the actual formal interview, but after the initial introductions have been made. It should give you a chance to gauge how the interviewee is feeling about the exchange, and to put everyone at ease (including yourself). This is not the time to bring out your recorder, camera or notepad, particularly if the interviewee appears uncertain about the exchange. This is also not the time to start asking questions or discussing areas that are critical to your interview. If your interviewee is still looking uncomfortable or threatened after your initial icebreaker, don't launch into your interview regardless. Keep the conversation going; even if this takes ten minutes or more, it will pay off in the end.

Beware, on the other hand, of wasting time – they might be nervous b/c they have an approaching deadline.

WHO?

If the interviewee is someone you call on frequently as a source, or is experienced in dealing with the news media, less time needs to be devoted to the icebreaker. Establishing a rapport is always important but busy people in public life value their time and expect an interview to be conducted quickly and efficiently. Unnecessary chit-chat will be seen as time-wasting and not conducive to an effective interview. Electronic journalists seeking a short news grab would rarely spend time on icebreakers, unless the person was inexperienced with the media.

Young people can be particularly difficult to interview. Often they are self-conscious and prone to one-word answers. Taking time to establish a rapport by asking 'easy' questions about their age, school and interests can give them the confidence to be more expansive in their interview answers. One feature writer recalled an interview with a shy 14-year-old athlete who was clearly nervous and reluctant to talk. 'I began with a series of questions about his age, what form he was in, how long he had been competing, the name of his coach. He found them easy to answer and loosened up a lot. The interview went well after that.'

CULTURAL CONCERNS

Cultural sensitivities must also be taken into account. For example, in New Zealand it is important to take time building up a relationship of trust with Maori contacts. According to Michael King, author of a (1985) guide to reporting Maori activities, it is rarely sufficient to make initial contact by telephone. You should have a preliminary face-to-face meeting with each major source to establish a rapport. A growing number of Maori newsmakers are now used to dealing with journalists but many remain unaware of how the media works, what is newsworthy and what is expected of them in interviews.

Similarly, members of Pacific Island communities who have been under-reported in the mainstream media will often be apprehensive, if not suspicious, of journalists. Explaining the purpose of the story and why the interview is essential can allay justified concerns and facilitate a successful interview.

Members of Aboriginal communities might be concerned the journalist only intends concentrating on negative stereotypes, and thus some time should be spent with the tribal Elders explaining the aim of the interview and how it will be used in the final story.

Dr Mina Roces of the University of New South Wales has conducted numerous interviews with Filipina women, often about quite sensitive and personal issues. She says she always begins by explaining the project and how the interviewee's help is invaluable. Dr Roces said one Filipina knew the interview was to be recorded on video, and had obviously been to the beauty parlour. 'I made sure I broke the ice by commenting on how lovely she looked' (personal interview with Dr Mina Roces, November 2000).

If you are interviewing someone from another culture it is essential, if you don't already have the background knowledge, to research conversational 'dos' and 'don'ts'. For instance, if you were interviewing someone from the Torres Strait Islands, you should find out exactly which island they are from—as each has its own diverse history and culture. If they are from Moa Island, for instance, get a map and find out exactly where it is, and research basic information about the island and its people before the interview. With Maori, it is important to establish their 'iwi' (tribe) and then show that you know where it is based. With Pacific Island and Asian communities it is essential to recognise and appreciate national identity and difference. Journalists who don't may cause offence.

RESEARCH ICEBREAKERS

Those who interview regularly agree that 'homework' always pays off when it comes to icebreakers, and in fact interviews as a whole. As Melbourne's *Herald Sun* associate editor John Hamilton points out: 'Say you're about to interview a public figure and you do your reading and you do your homework and you find, for example, in a small cutting somewhere that the person reads science fiction. If you just pop this into the conversation and say: "I understand you've got an interest in science fiction?" they go "Crikey, you know a bit about me". It flatters them, and people respond to flattery' (personal interview with John Hamilton, November 2000).

Understandably the interviewee would be impressed that you have gone to the trouble to find out about them and their interests. A similar instance many years ago involved a radio journalist who had to interview a conservationist and television personality about a talk he was giving on sustainable development (not a common topic at the time). The journalist read widely, including getting a copy of the talk from the last venue where the interviewee had spoken. The subject had planned to talk for about 15 minutes but, when he realised the journalist had gone to some trouble (and actually said as much to the journalist), the interview continued for almost 2 hours.

If you know someone is interested in surfing, skiing, photography or any other sport or recreation, this can be very useful, particularly if you share the interest and can talk knowledgeably about it. If you keep up-to-date with current affairs (which should always be the case with journalists), you could comment on a recent issue or event to break the ice. Be wary about making political comments, though, as this could have the reverse effect and make the atmosphere very frosty. It may also set you up for accusations of bias.

You and the interviewee may have a mutual friend/acquaintance/colleague and a greeting from them will certainly get things started on a good note. Again a word of caution: ensure that they are definitely on friendly terms before you start name dropping. Another way to shut down an interview is to express doubt or disapproval. Making a judgemental response will probably cause offence. Equally, you should not be disingenuous and make false expressions of approval. The best approach is to be as objective as possible.

ON-THE-SPOT ICEBREAKERS

Unfortunately you do not always have the time to research the subject of an interview, particularly if it is the result of a spontaneous event or an unexpected opportunity. This is when you must call on your general knowledge or powers of observation to formulate on-the-spot icebreakers. If all else fails, comment on the weather, but this is definitely a last resort.

Regularly described as one of Australian television's best interviewers, Andrew Urban is a master of the icebreaker. In the SBS television series 'Front Up' he literally 'fronts up' to people on the street, in cafes and other assorted locations and starts talking to them. In a very short time Andrew is able to put the

Master of the icebreaker Andrew Urban (right) *with cameraman Greg Kay, recording interviews for 'Front Up'.*
(Photo by Louise Keller, courtesy of SBS Publicity)

interviewees so at ease that they reveal a variety of aspects about their public and private lives.

Because he has never met the interviewees before—in fact he does not even know their names until he approaches them—Andrew relies totally on his powers of observation. For instance, if he sees someone polishing the brass on their boat at the marina, the icebreaker will be based on the boat, and may eventually include a request to come aboard and take a closer look. The same goes for motorcycles, bicycles, books, tattoos, bags of shopping and a continually changing assortment of conversation starters.

Andrew says you need to establish a rapport before the interview can begin—and the key is to start with something that the subject is comfortable with.

> It's not important what it is—just a very general question. For instance: 'Why are you wearing a purple top?'. And you might reply: 'Because it's my mother's favourite colour'. And that would lead me into asking about your mother, and get the conversation started in a non-threatening way (personal interview with Andrew Urban, April 2000).

The *Herald Sun*'s John Hamilton looks at the surroundings for inspiration for on-the-spot icebreakers.

> For example if I'm going to somebody's home to do an interview, one of the first things I do is look at the garden as I walk up the path. Because if they're keen gardeners they might have beautiful roses . . . it's a conversation point for a start. When you walk up and you're meeting a stranger at the front door you can say 'What wonderful roses, isn't that a Peace over there?' (I don't know many roses) and they usually say, 'No, it's a Queen Victoria' and so you get a conversation going (personal interview with John Hamilton, November 2000).

*John Hamilton, with Dame Elisabeth Murdoch, uses the surroundings
of her property, Cruden Farm, for an on-the-spot icebreaker.*
(Photo by Craig Borrow, courtesy of the *Herald Sun*)

Once you're inside their home, there are good opportunities for
further icebreakers, as the surroundings tend to reflect the sort
of person they are. Items such as ornaments, paintings, photographs and sporting trophies are obvious conversation starters.
Pets are a particularly easy way to get acquainted, especially
if you share their passion for cats/dogs/birds/snakes. John
Hamilton believes a great clue to a person is books.

> Books on the shelf or books they are currently reading. Not
> only are these books good conversation starters, but they
> help to build a picture of the person you are talking to,
> which is particularly helpful for feature pieces (personal
> interview with John Hamilton, November 2000).

If you're in an office you might comment on the view (if
there is one), but if the location is neutral perhaps you might

comment on their jewellery, their watch, or some other personal effect. Avoid concentrating too much on their personal appearance though. Andrew Urban will often use appearance as an icebreaker, but stresses you must approach the topic in a positive way.

> For instance you don't say:'Where did you get that ridiculous haircut from?' and still expect the person to be willing to continue. However, I would say something like: 'That's an interesting haircut. Can you tell me a little bit about that?', in a positive tone, making it obvious I was curious but not critical (personal interview with Andrew Urban, April 2000).

Studio locations can be daunting and a good way to break the ice is to empathise with the talent's nervousness. Make a joke about how hot the lights get in a television studio, or how all the equipment in the radio studio scares most journalists. This is the one time where the interviewer can talk about their experiences and background, using it as a way to put the interviewee at ease.

One radio journalist started a difficult interview by confessing her (genuine) fear of all the studio equipment and some of her early mistakes. It not only showed a more personal side to the journalist, but also broke the ice with a few laughs. No matter what technique you use for your icebreaker, there is no substitute for genuine interest and enthusiasm. There are not too many people who do not enjoy telling their story, particularly to a good listener. Make sure it is obvious right from the start that you want to hear their story.

Australian journalist Peter Davis recalled an encounter where the icebreaker made the difference between getting the interview and going back to work empty-handed. 'I was interviewing Dr Arthur C. Clarke at his home in Colombo. I had always been a bit of a fan of the world famous scientist and science fiction writer—ever since I went to the opening night of *2001* in London. I had gathered by way of research (from other journos) that if he didn't like you his eyes would simply glaze over and he would gesture to the door and wait for you to leave.'

When I finally met up with him I was ushered into the office of his mansion. He seemed brisk and short. 'Come in, come in,' he said. 'Now what exactly is it you want to know?' He asked the question even before I was sitting down and before I had the chance to observe the room. I knew that in that nanosecond I could either win or lose him. I noticed his computer in the corner and a huge picture of a telescope on his wall. All the questions I had so carefully prepared vanished from my mind. I was almost completely blank. Then, without thinking, I asked, 'Do you reckon the Hubble space telescope can be rescued?' His eyes lit up like an overzealous schoolboy, he lurched at his computer and showed me the letter he'd written to the NASA Space Administration just two days earlier, outlining his theories about how Hubble could indeed be rescued. Two hours later we were still engrossed in conversation and I knew I had a good story (personal interview with Peter Davis, June 2000).

TIPS:

- Do your homework
- Choose something from your research, but not an area critical to the actual interview

---

- Good on-the-spot icebreakers can involve remarks about books, the garden, trophies, paintings, pets or photographs
- Keep up-to-date with current affairs as a way of breaking the ice
- Know cultural 'dos' and 'don'ts'
- Don't be too personal: an interesting watch or piece of jewellery should be reasonably safe
- The last resort—comment on the weather!

REFERENCES

Biagi, S. 1986, *Interviews that Work: A Practical Guide for Journalists*, Wadsworth Publishing Company, Belmont, California

King, M. 1985, *Kawe Korero—A Guide to Reporting Maori Activities*, New Zealand Journalists Training Board, Wellington

Metzler, K. 1977, *Creative Interviewing: The Writer's Guide to Gathering Information by Asking Questions*, Prentice-Hall Inc., New Jersey

Personal interview with Peter Davis, June 2000

Personal interview with John Hamilton, November 2000

Personal interview with Kerry O'Brien, November 2000

Personal interview with Dr Mina Roces, November 2000

Personal interview with Andrew Urban, April 2000

5

THE QUESTIONS

A cadet journalist recalling one of her very first interviews with an overwhelming businessman said she hadn't prepared very well and was too afraid to ask any questions. After waiting a few minutes while she fumbled around trying to get started, the businessman asked, 'Do you take shorthand?', to which the journalist replied, 'Yes.' 'Well, take this down then,' he said, and then proceeded to dictate a story to the journalist, including quotes and full punctuation . . . right down to the very last full stop. It was a hard lesson, but the journalist said she always comes completely prepared now . . . and she always asks questions no matter how daunting the interviewee.

Though it can be difficult sometimes, you must always ask questions, otherwise you could be treated as a secretary taking down a prepared speech. Your preparation time should include your background research, as well as thinking through your questions and writing them down. Australian political journalist

Kerry O'Brien believes that you should always write down your questions because:

> Questions help you to focus your attention on the essence of the story or interview. They also help you to order your thoughts in a logical flow, and in framing the question you are also endeavouring to think through what kind of answer the person will give. And that then becomes part of the flow into the next question (personal interview with Kerry O'Brien, November 2000).

However, Kerry warns:

> Many interviewers before me have talked about the trap of sticking to your questions regardless of the answers. And even though you've got your questions prepared, and even though a part of you (whether you like it or not) will be thinking about what you're going to ask next, you've also got to be listening to the answers, and you've got to be processing the answers as you go. You've got to be prepared to throw your questions to one side, or even move from Question 2 to Question 6, because of something that the interviewee has said that demands logically that you go to Question 6. Then you might have to retrace back to Question 4 rather than Question 3, or you might be jettisoning Question 3 altogether (personal interview with Kerry O'Brien, November 2000).

All stories—whether hard or soft news—should answer six essential questions. These are commonly called the five Ws and one H—or the Who, What, When, Where, Why and How questions. Every story, no matter how brief, should provide answers to the Who, What, When and Where questions, while longer investigative pieces, or current affairs stories, tackle the Why and How. Kerry O'Brien believes the 'old fundamentals' (the five Ws and one H) will almost always get you through.

> If you come back from any assignment and haven't answered those—to some degree at least—then I hope it's because people have refused to give it to you, not because you have failed to ask (personal interview with Kerry O'Brien, November 2000).

He also feels it's important to understand the difference between what people want to say and what you, on behalf of your audience, should be getting from them.

> I think it's valid enough for many people to be seeking to use various media outlets as a forum for their ideas, but equally they should expect and understand that it's your job as a journalist to be there on behalf of the audience, not to help them. So if they've got interesting, important things to say without too much prodding on your part—fine. If you can vouch for the veracity of it, the essential truth of it, fine. But in many instances you've got to be there as the check and balance of what's being said. You're not a cipher, you're not somebody's platform, you're not just there for someone to stand on and cast their message out unchecked. I think the bulk of people will want you to show some respect, they'll want you to show common courtesies, but they also want you to be their representative asking the tough questions and keeping people honest.
>
> You're there as the vehicle for the flow of information— but not an unquestioning vehicle (personal interview with Kerry O'Brien, November 2000).

Whether you are reporting for a news brief or a cover story, you should always be interested in your interviewee—and show it. This should be clear in both your verbal and non-verbal techniques. The simple technique of asking informed questions then listening to the answers for cues for the next question is the best way to display interest. Questioning techniques can be divided into three main areas:

1. Questions to use
2. Questions to try
3. Questions to avoid

Case study: To explore these various techniques we will use the example of an interview with a bank official conducting a tour of small country branches.

DO ASK the 'who cares' question

One of the essential news values is *consequence*—in other words a story must be significant or impact on people to be newsworthy. Generally the more people who are affected by a story, the larger the story and the closer it will appear to the top of the bulletin or to page 1 of the newspaper. News editors will apply the 'who cares' principle when deciding where your story will be placed and how long it will be, so you should have the answer when you return from the interview. With the bank story it would be essential to determine not only how many branches would be involved in the tour, but also the extent of the region (including population) that would be affected if any changes were made as a result of the visit.

Which can be gotten from research or from underlings.

EXAMPLES

Q: You're visiting 30 branches. How many people are employed in total?

Q: What are the major regions serviced?

Q: How many customers are involved?

DO USE closed questions but not too often

These are the questions that require only a very limited response—usually a 'yes' or 'no'.

Examples

Q: Have you conducted a tour like this before?

Q: Have you been to these areas before?

If your subject is not particularly forthcoming and is inclined towards giving short answers using closed questions will not help. Generally journalists are discouraged from using closed questions, but they can come in handy if you want a definitive answer. During the interview with the bank official visiting the branches, it would be useful to ask: 'Are you going to close any branches as a result of your tour?' If the answer is 'no', it should be kept on record in case there is a change of heart in the future. If the answer is 'yes', you have a front page story.

DO USE open questions for more information

Closed questions are easily converted into open questions—the sort of questions that require more than a yes or no answer. By the simple addition of one of the six essential questions (Who, What, When, Where, Why, and How), the question is opened up and should ensure longer answers.

Example

The closed question:

Q: Do you hope to visit a number of branches during your tour?

(that would probably only elicit a yes or no answer) is easily converted into six open questions which ask for longer and more interesting responses.

Q: *Who* will you meet during the tour?
Q: *What* do you hope to achieve?
Q: *When* will you be touring?
Q: *Where* will your tour take you?
Q: *How* will this benefit the public?
Q: *Why* have you chosen this region?

The 'how' and the 'why' questions will generally elicit the most in-depth information and are usually saved for more investigative pieces or longer current affairs stories.

DO USE short precise questions that are easy to answer

American journalist and author of *Interviews that Work* (1986), Shirley Biagi says questions that are longer than three lines are too long. Unless some background explanation is required, three lines is a maximum—particularly for broadcast interviews. In fact, the shorter the better. A sage piece of advice given to a print journalist moving into radio was that the audience has tuned in to hear the person being interviewed—not the journalist. This is also the case with print interviews—the interviewee should not have to interrupt the interviewer to make a response. Some broadcast journalists have been known to ask questions of more than 45 seconds—sometimes up to 1 minute. This is far too long.

Example

Instead of asking:

Q: This bank tour is said to be far more extensive than others that have been conducted in the past, which have not resulted in any significant changes and have just been fact-finding missions with no outcomes. What results do you expect from this tour?

Why not ask:

Q: What results do you expect this time?

DO USE the 'bigger, brighter, better' question

A lot of interviews should present 'must ask' questions for the journalist. These are the sort of questions the public would want to ask if they were conducting the interview themselves. For instance, an interview with a police detective about a drug raid invites the 'bigger, brighter, better' question. The curious journalist should be wondering: what makes this raid different, special, unusual or worthy of coverage?; what gives it that news-worthy angle? If these questions are forgotten a good angle is lost.

Example

Q: Is this the biggest drug raid in this area/state/country?

A 'yes' answer to this question could easily result in a front page story.

DO USE the challenge or investigative question

Many answers, particularly those given by people used to dealing with the media, should not go unchallenged. However if you do want to investigate an answer it is advisable to do your research first.

Do research to ask better Qs!

Example

For instance, let's say the bank official answered your closed question—Are you going to close any branches as a result of your tour?—with a definite 'no'. However, your research found that a similar tour five years earlier resulted in the closure of four branches and the loss of fifteen jobs. Knowing this you *must* ask:

Q: When you toured five years ago you also promised no closures or job losses. Four branches were closed and fifteen people retrenched. What makes this time different?

The official will either explain the difference, if there is one, or ask for the evidence that backs up your 'statement question'. You must be able to provide this. Without proof a statement like this could get you into a lot of trouble, or leave you looking foolish.

DO USE a summary for more information

This technique requires the interviewee to agree or disagree with information you have summarised. As a device to clarify and sometimes to extract a definitive answer, the summary can be a very efficient tool. Instead of getting a 'yes' or 'no' to just one closed question, the summary contains much more information to which the interviewee either agrees or disagrees. Australian journalist Jana Wendt used this technique very effectively in an interview with media owner Rupert Murdoch on the first edition of Channel 7's former current affairs program 'Witness'. She used summarisation to clarify the current position of business dealings being conducted between Murdoch and rival media tycoon Kerry Packer. At the height of the Super League battle (caused by Rupert Murdoch's proposal of a 'super' league which split the existing league, then merged with the ARL to form the NRL) Packer had agreed to help make the peace within rugby league in Australia in return for some broadcast rights and access to Murdoch's Fox movies for his Nine Network.

> JW: Let me talk then about this arrangement, this deal that you had with Mr Packer, or thought you had. Did you shake hands on this deal?
> RM: Of course.
> . . .
> JW: But if I can just summarise your view of it, since Mr Packer did not deliver on his side of the bargain, presumably you don't want to deliver on your side?
> RM: I think that would be a fair summarisation, yes
> (Channel 7, 9 April 1996).

DO USE questions that ask for summaries, rankings or choices

An excellent way to obtain more definitive answers is to ask the interviewee to provide their own summary, to rank information they have been given, or to make a choice. Not only does this provide more detail, but it also gives their order of priority or importance.

Examples

For instance, the bank official could be asked for a summary:

Q: Could you summarise the main reasons for this tour?

Then to rank the summary:

Q: Could you put those four reasons in order of importance for your company?

And then to make a choice:

Q: What do you believe is the most important reason for looking at these country branches?

DO USE requests for clarification by repeating the answer

The best interviews are the ones where journalists are listening intently, then using the interviewee's answers to lead into the next question. Taking this point even further, the actual words of the answer can be used to formulate the next question. This is a useful technique for ensuring that you have heard correctly, and for stressing the importance of the answer.

Example

In the interview with the bank official visiting the country branches try:

Q: What changes do you expect to result from your report?

A: I expect there could be changes in staffing levels and the services provided.

Q: Staffing levels could be changed. How?

DO USE

- The 'who cares' question
- Closed questions (but not too often)
- Open questions for more information
- Short precise questions that are easy to answer
- The 'bigger, brighter, better' question
- The challenge or investigative question
- A summary for more information
- Questions that ask for summaries, rankings or choices
- Requests for clarification by repeating the answer

DO TRY repeating or rephrasing questions

Repeating or rewording questions may work on the interviewee who doesn't deal with the media very often, but politicians and business leaders pick up on this technique very quickly. They are just as likely to point out that it doesn't matter how many times you repeat the question, or rephrase it, they are not going to answer.

Examples

Q: You said staffing levels could change as a result of the study. How?

A: I really can't answer that until it has been conducted.

Q: Are you trying to say that staff may be put off?

A: No, I'm not saying that at all. I can't say what will happen until we look at the branches.

Q: Do you have any indication that the branches in this region are overstaffed?

A: Again, no, not until we do the research.

Political journalist Kerry O'Brien believes if you're confident of your topic, which generally comes from preparation, repeating questions is a valid technique.

Whether it's the Prime Minister, the Opposition Leader or the Treasurer, they are, in the end, also only people. They have their own insecurities, and their own doubts, as well as their own confidence. Yes, they come armed with media skills that have been well honed over years, and yes, they have the capacity to sidetrack, and to spindoctor, and all of these other things. But if you have listened carefully to the answers, and it is clear to you that they have not answered your questions, then even though you feel that you're a junior journalist and they're a heavyweight, you can, in a reasonable tone, point out that they haven't answered the question. You can say 'Could I just remind you of what the question was?' without being aggressive (personal interview with Kerry O'Brien, November 2000).

What info (exact or type) were you reaching for? Did you get it? No? Rephrase.

If your interviewee does not understand your question, they may ask you to reword it, or to clarify what you want. This may mean your questions are too wordy. Remember: the interview is not a contest, it is a means of obtaining information from a source for publication. Don't make it too difficult, either for the interviewee or your audience, by using complex words, jargon or overly long statements or questions.

DO TRY posing a hypothetical question

Most interviewees would have difficulty answering the hypothetical question, and many will refuse to tackle a problem that may never arise. Those who have attended 'managing the media' sessions are trained to refuse to answer these questions.

Example

For instance, with our bank official, you might try:

Q: What will you do if bank staff around the country go on strike as a result of your recommendations?

But the official is likely to answer:

A: I think this is a highly unlikely scenario, which I'd prefer not to discuss.

DO TRY playing the devil's advocate

While you may agree with the interviewee, it is a useful technique to challenge them and their answers. This provides the opportunity for a more balanced coverage of the issue. Quite often you can state quite clearly what you are doing:

Example

Q: If I could just play the devil's advocate here . . . Don't you think the criteria you are using to judge the viability of the branches is unfair?

Kerry O'Brien believes playing devil's advocate is a good approach to an interview.

> You don't have to be aggressive about it. If it's a politician or an advocate for any cause, I think it's important for an audience to feel that these people's claims have been tested. That's part of what you're there for. And obviously you can't really test a person unless you've got some understanding of what they're talking about—which goes back to your research and preparation (personal interview with Kerry O'Brien, November 2000).

DO TRY the tough question

Asking the tough question—or dropping the bomb—is not for the first-time interviewer or the faint hearted. It

Paul Lyneham,
courtesy of the Nine Network.

is difficult asking the hard question, but most journalists feel it is only fair to give the interviewee the opportunity to give their side of the story, or to answer criticism.

The late Paul Lyneham, an award-winning television journalist, believed it could be very difficult asking the hard question, but essential when you feel an injustice has been done or that the interviewee has a case to answer. In the following anecdote, he recalled one instance of how he coped with asking the difficult question.

My most famous recollection of that dilemma was a story I was doing for 'Four Corners' and we spent three days filming at a notoriously Dickensian cheese factory for a story about migrant women workers. We talked our way in there on the basis of doing a story about the factory. Of course in that situation you delay the real interview until the very last minute, so you go around the factory, get all the shots of the women working standing up when they could have been sitting down, and carrying big boxes of cheese over slimy floors.

The man who owned the factory thought this was the best thing that had ever happened to him because he was going to get all this publicity on national television. And he took us out to lunch, and gave us the five-star treatment, you know, and thought I was his brother, and there was going to come the inevitable moment of deep and thorough-going betrayal—from his point of view anyway.

Ethical?

From my point of view, I thought he had a really substantive case to answer in terms of the way he was treating his workforce, but I also had to be prepared for the fact that he'd bolt when he realised what was happening and there was no way apart from having a firm response ready.

So I said to him—and this was a real dry-throat breathless sort of anxiety thing because I was looking him right in the eye—I mean if you're going to stab anybody, you know, it takes extra guts to do it right in the front.

And I said, 'Tell me what section of what award entitles you to get these women to clean your Rolls-Royce at lunch time'.

Which I thought set the tone of the interview fairly clearly, and he tried to get out of the chair and I mean that would have had a certain dramatic appeal, except we hadn't really got the interview going. And what could I do about it? Nothing. Except to wag my finger at him and say very sternly 'Why don't you just sit there and answer the questions?' Which is something I've never done ever before or since, and it worked. And he sat there . . . like a little boy, and in the end, on the first cut of the documentary I didn't run terribly much of him because I thought he almost looked like a figure of the underdog, but then others thought I was being a bit too sensitive.

But that's the great occasion when I've really choked, and had to say to myself, come on, let's get real, let's get on with it (personal interview with Paul Lyneham, April 1996).

DO TRY the 'how does it feel' question—sparingly

This question is overdone by the media, appears to be asking the obvious, and is the one question the public complains that it hears far too often. The journalist who asks the champion swimmer, 'How does it feel to have made the Olympic team?' does not expect them to say 'It feels terrible'. Put more thought into this question if you want to use it. You could ask the swimmer: 'What was the best feeling—knowing you had made the Olympic team, or that you had broken the world record?'.

Despite its overuse, the 'How does it feel?' question will almost always work in a positive situation, as with the swimmer. However caution must be used if you decide to ask this question in less happy circumstances.

For instance, the television journalist who asks recently bereaved parents: 'How does it feel to know you will never see your child again?' cannot expect them to be very forthcoming.

This sort of question can also be used as an aggressive device, but you must be prepared to hold your ground if the interviewee becomes defensive.

Example

For instance, with the bank official, you could try:

Q: How does it feel to have the fate of the staff in this region in your hands?

However, don't be surprised if the official becomes less than helpful after you ask this.

Most examples here are too aggressive.

DO TRY projection

To soften the difficult question, or to reduce hostility in the interview, journalists often project accusations to a third party—'some people might say' or 'your critics might ask'. The most famous example of using this technique—and seeing it go wrong—is the much repeated 1981 interview between former British Prime Minister Margaret Thatcher and George Negus (who was a journalist for Channel 9's '60 Minutes' at the time).

GN: Why do people stop us in the street almost and tell us that Margaret Thatcher isn't just inflexible, she's not just single minded, on occasions she's just plain pig headed and won't be told by anyone?

MT: Would you tell me who has stopped you in the street and said that?

GN: Ordinary Britons.

MT: Where?

GN: In conversation, in pubs.

MT (Interrupting): I thought you'd just come from Belize.

GN: Oh, it's not the first time we've been here.

MT: Will you tell me who and where and when?

GN: Ordinary Britons in restaurants and cabs.

MT: How many?

GN: I would say at least one in two.

MT: I'm sorry, it's an expression that I've never heard . . . tell me who has said it to you, when and where?

(Little 1994: 23-4)

Of course, Negus couldn't. While this exchange was described as 'good television' it should serve as a warning if you plan to make use of the projection technique.

DO TRY the 'dumb' or innocent question

Asking the innocent or 'dumb' question such as 'I don't really understand this, could you explain it to me?' can work very well, particularly in getting the interviewee to explain something in simpler terms more suited for the publication or broadcast. It is also a useful device to get the interviewee to reveal more information.

Example

With the bank official, you could ask:

Q: I'm sorry, I don't quite understand. Could you explain how you decide if a branch is viable?

However the journalist at an international press conference following a major basketball tournament took this technique a little bit too far when he asked:'Could you tell me please why you get two points when you score a goal?'

DO TRY the leading question

This technique is used as a way of getting the interviewee to use your words in their answer. It may work if the interviewee agrees with what you are saying, but otherwise it is rare that your lead will be used.

Example

For instance, it is unlikely the interviewee will use any of the words from the following question, as they would not want to repeat any negative ideas.

Q: Could this tour be seen as just another way of penalising people for living outside metropolitan centres?

However, if you asked:

Q: Is this tour one way of ensuring customers have the services they require?

The interviewee may well answer:

A: Yes, this is the major way we ensure regional customers have the services they require.

DO TRY the trick question

Sometimes a question can be worded in such a way that the interviewee will be trapped if they attempt to answer it. This technique is generally used with those who are trained in dealing with the media and is either left unanswered, or the answer may be that they have recognised the trick. It may work, but it is rare when it does.

Example

Q: Don't you feel it is unfair to look at reducing services in this region?

Whichever way the bank official answers—yes or no—it will be a confirmation that services are being reduced, so a savvy interviewee would deflect this question.

DO TRY

- Repeating or rewording questions
- Posing a hypothetical question
- Playing the devil's advocate
- The tough question

DO TRY

- The 'how does it feel' question—sparingly
- Projection
- The 'dumb' or innocent question
- The leading question
- The trick question

DON'T ASK double- or triple-barrelled questions

Questions that are 'two in one' or even 'three in one' are confusing for even the best and most practised interviewees. If a journalist asks a long triple-barrelled question, the interviewee would be likely to choose either the easiest question of the three, or the last question. Some interviewees are so proficient at interviews that they will answer all three, but this sort of ability is rare.

Example

Don't ask the bank official:

Q: Do you plan to close bank branches as a result of this tour, and will this be the first time you have conducted a tour such as this?

It would be an unusually rare and forthcoming interviewee who would answer the first question when given the option.

DON'T ASK the 'tell me all about yourself' question—unless specific

This is an incredibly lazy question and everyone knows it, even someone who is rarely interviewed. One journalist asked this exact question at the start of an interview with a university professor. The professor handed him a CV and told him to come back when he had some 'real' questions to ask.

Another example involved a press conference with actor Robert Carlyle and a group of international journalists.

> He seemed to be warming up and ready to talk about his recent big life shock—a newspaper tracking down the mother he hadn't seen for 30 years since she walked out on him when he was a small boy— when a German journalist took the floor. 'Robert,' he said, 'please, I have never heard of you before. Tell me about what other things you have done' (Williams 1997: 14).

Sometimes the 'tell me about yourself' question is used in feature interviews, but usually in reference to a more specific timeframe or situation, such as, 'Tell me what it was like when you heard about your father's death', or 'Tell me all about yourself when you decided to travel to India'.

DON'T ASK

- Double- or triple-barrelled questions
- The 'tell me all about yourself' question—unless in relation to a specific event or time

---

DO KEEP in focus and in control

One of the most important elements of an interview, and often the most difficult, is maintaining control. Some journalists will rise to the bait and start verbal sparring with the interviewee. All this does is get the interviewee off the hook, while the journalist loses control, their cool and—in the case of broadcast journalists—the respect of the audience.

In her interview with media tycoon Rupert Murdoch, Jana Wendt admirably maintains her cool after some very personal barbs are sent her way. She keeps the focus and continues on with the interview despite several attempts of provocation. The interview is primarily about Murdoch's attempts to set up Super League. In the following segment Murdoch appears to be trying to take control of the interview by posing a question to Wendt, and then attempts to bait her about 'astronomical salaries'. Wendt continues with her line of questioning, and eventually Murdoch, who had been denying the large offers of money, agrees with Wendt's original statement.

RM: Why were they so loyal to us?
JW: Money?

RM: No. They get money—they were offered other money.

JW: They were offered astronomical amounts of money by you.

RM: Well, not by your standards. (smiles)

JW: Astronomical amounts of money by any standards. Multiples of their salaries previously.

RM: No, I don't know about that. It depends who and what and what the bidding was, and so on. Some, sure, I mean some were going to be paid properly (Channel 7's 'Witness', 9 April 1996).

Above all—try to avoid the obvious. For instance, the journalist who asked the two members of the popular singing group sister2sister, 'How did you meet?' should probably go back to the drawing board.

Learn what you can ahead of time.

REFERENCES

Biagi, S. 1986, *Interviews That Work: A Practical Guide for Journalists*, Wadsworth Publishing Company, California

Channel 7 1996, Interview by Jana Wendt with Rupert Murdoch, 'Witness', 9 April 1996

Jervis, B. 1989, *News Sense*, Advertiser Newspapers Limited, Adelaide

Little, J. 1994, *60 Minutes*, Allen & Unwin, St Leonards

Personal interview with Paul Lyneham, April 1996

Personal interview with Kerry O'Brien, November 2000

Williams, S. 1997, 'Interviews: the stupid in pursuit of the irrelevant', *The Australian*, 23 April 1997, p. 14

6

PRINT INTERVIEWS

Andrea Carson, industrial reporter for Melbourne's *The Age*, says she still uses the two pieces of advice she was given about interviewing when she first started working as a print journalist—to re-check details such as title and spelling of name, and to ask if the interviewee wanted to add anything that hadn't been covered. 'The first piece of advice avoided a lot of errors, and the second often resulted in a really good angle coming up at the end of the interview, with them talking about an area I had not thought to ask about' (personal interview with Andrea Carson, October 2000).

Print news interviews can be divided into two major categories: hard news (which is usually spot news or news of the day and heavily fact-reliant); and soft news (which is timeless material featuring people, celebrities or issues). There are also many variations within these categories that govern the length of the interview and the techniques used. The hard news interview could be seeking the latest facts for anything from a three-paragraph news brief about a road accident to a major cover story exposing corruption. The soft news interview focuses on the human interest angles (or the emotions), and is very often for a personality piece (a feature story about a person).

The hard news brief requires the journalist to concentrate on the basic questions (Who, What, When and Where) and generally is about 'who said what' or 'who did what'. The investigative story also seeks these basic facts, but must extend the interview to obtain comment and opinion—aiming to discover the 'Why' and 'How' of the issue. While also seeking facts and quotes, the personality piece concentrates on 'softer' angles designed to appeal to the emotions.

Australian political journalist Kerry O'Brien says when you're doing a hard news interview the questions are fairly self-evident, but that you should 'cast your net' in feature interviews.

> If it's a road accident: What were the conditions? What caused it? What was the state of the road? Was the driver DUI? [driving under the influence]. Those things are obvious. However when I was doing features for newspapers you would tend to cast your net a bit. You could be somewhat more conversational in the way you put the questions. As a newspaper journalist I've got no doubt I was much less disciplined as an interviewer than I am now. Provided the person on the other side of the desk was willing, you could sit for an hour doing what you might have 15 minutes to do, or 10 minutes to do in television, and then you could go back at your own pace and distil it all down and work it all through (personal interview with Kerry O'Brien, November 2000).

There is no set formula for conducting any of these interviews, but there are some essential steps that should be carried out before, during and after the exchange. To demonstrate these steps we use an interview with Jon Coyne, a bank official conducting a tour of small country branches, as an example. The first interview is a hard news piece and incorporates interviewing for fact and opinion, while the second interview is a feature profile piece on the bank official.

Each case study details fifteen essential steps for a print interview. Chapters 2 and 3 of this book provide full details about these steps.

CASE STUDY 1—Hard news interview for fact and opinion—fifteen key steps

While the following case study includes steps for conducting a hard news interview, the list below, and its order of presentation, is not prescriptive. Every interview you conduct will be different and should be treated as such.

1. Arrange an interview time and place
2. Do your research
3. Organise your questions or keywords
4. Organise your notepad and equipment
5. Arrive at the interview early
6. Get set up and check your equipment again
7. Ask your icebreaker question
8. Explain the purpose of the interview
9. Ask your first interview question
10. Ask the What, When, Where and Who questions
11. Ask the comment or opinion questions
12. Listen

13. Ask the 'who cares' or 'who will be affected' question
14. Follow up with the challenge or investigative question
15. Check your notes

Don't forget to thank the interviewee for their valuable time after you have completed these steps.

Fifteen key steps in detail

1. Arrange an interview time and place. The venue can play a major role in the success or otherwise of an interview. Choosing a quiet spot is particularly important for a broadcast interview that is being recorded. A quiet spot is also helpful for a print interview as it can be difficult to concentrate and decipher your notes on a busy thoroughfare or in a bustling café. Choosing a suitable time can also be important, particularly with busy interviewees. If you choose a time on the hour— such as 4 pm—the interviewee may well perceive it as an open-ended slot (at least for 1 hour anyway), and be unwilling to commit to this amount of time. However, if you choose 3.45 pm, or even 3.30 pm, it appears as though you have confined the interview to a shorter time—between 15 and 30 minutes respectively. This first step should also be the time when you introduce yourself and your organisation, and ensure the interviewee knows the interview will be on the record and for publication. Confirm all arrangements (date, time and place) at the end of this step.

2. Do your research. Even if you only have a short time before the interview, use it for research. The more you can find out about the person and the issue, the better the interview result. Author and journalist Shirley Biagi believes 'the ideal situation is to have weeks for research before an interview and weeks to write the story afterward. But this is a fantasy. Reporters usually write an interview story the day they do the interview' (1986: 3).

3. Organise and write down your questions. Actually writing down your questions will help you focus your attention on the issue or person. These could be written on one page of your notepad. Before you organise your questions you should summarise the purpose or 'angle' of your interview. If you cannot do this in less than 30 words, it's back to the drawing board. You should have a clear and concise idea of what you want from the interview, but don't be afraid to deviate if new angles appear.

4. Organise your notepad and equipment. There's nothing more embarrassing than having your one and only pen run out halfway through an interview. Of course any equipment used in the print interview— probably a mini-disc recorder or tape recorder (and perhaps a digital camera for photographs)—should be checked and re-checked before an interview.

5. Arrive at the interview early. Early is good—but no more than about five minutes. If you arrive much earlier than that it puts pressure on the interviewee to finish what they are doing sooner than they had planned, and your super-punctuality may not be appreciated.

6. Get set up and check your equipment again. In these few minutes before the interview get set up and comfortable. If the interviewee is not conversant with media interviews, you may want to wait until you have progressed through your icebreaker before you bring out any recorders (or even your notepad).

7. Ask your icebreaker question. This is where your research is essential in providing an area of interest to use for the icebreaker. If you do not have the luxury of this preparation, you may well comment on the surroundings or something in the news that day. If all else fails, talk about the weather.

8. Explain the purpose of the interview. Start your interview by explaining what you are hoping to achieve, and where and when the story is likely to be used. Do not give a guarantee that it will be used in the next edition of the newspaper, as a major story may break, pushing yours out.

9. Ask your first question. With print interviews you usually have the time to ask your easy questions first, working up to the 'tough' questions or 'bombs'. The correct title and spelling of the interviewee's name should be number one on your list. Remember: don't assume anything. Even if your interviewee's name is 'John Coin', you cannot assume the usual spelling of these names. 'John' could be spelt 'Jon', or 'Jonn' or 'Johnn'. At this point don't forget to request their preferred title.

TIP:

Please do not take this advice too literally—some cadet journalists have even asked Prime Ministers to spell their names!

---

10. Ask the What, When, Where and Who questions. While the subject of the interview is generally the 'Who', quite often they are involved with others in the context of the story. In this case you would need to clarify which bank branches were to be included in the audit and the customers who could be affected. Jon Coyne, the bank staff and the customers are the 'Who' in this story.

11. Ask the comment ('How') or opinion ('Why') questions. In this story the 'Why' is particularly critical. You should ask questions such as: 'Why is the audit being conducted in this region?', 'Why have these particular branches been chosen?' and 'How will this affect farmers in the region?'

12. Listen. Definitely worth a section on its own. It should be understood that you are observing and listening throughout the whole interview—listening to answers and ensuring their body language is in synch with their verbal responses. Listening is critical, and in fact may produce totally unexpected results. If an answer deviates from your list of questions, make sure you note it down, together with a small question or keyword nearby to make sense of the answer. For example, on checking your notes to write the story you may find the answer: 'Definitely, that's what we intend to do'. You know it's critical because you've put a star beside it, but you can't recall the question that prompted the response.

13. Ask the 'who cares' or 'who will be affected' question. This is a critical question and could determine the prominence of the story when published. For instance if, through questioning, you were able to find out that the audit was going to result in a reduction of jobs and services, it may well make page 1 of the newspaper. This is because there is a large group of people 'who care' and will be affected by, or interested in, this story. Generally the larger the group, the more prominent the story (placement and size). So any story that the editor believes has a high percentage of readers 'who care' will be placed in a prominent position, such as pages one or three, and may fill the whole page. Those judged to have a smaller interested readership will take up less space and may be relegated to the back pages.

14. Follow up with the challenge or investigative question. Time for the 'bomb' or tough question. In this particular interview the tough question may well be the same as the 'who cares' question. This should be left until the end of the interview. If the interviewee handles this question well, then continue with some softer questions, before dropping another 'bomb'. If you don't get suitable answers—ones that you can easily understand—or ones that your readers will easily understand—ask again. This applies to all your questions.

15. Check your notes. If you have covered all the areas you had planned in your interview, now is the time to check through your notes. Explain to the interviewee that you are checking to ensure you have all the information you need. Most interviewees would prefer to spend a couple of minutes at the end of the interview while you check your notes, rather than receive a number of follow-up telephone calls or emails chasing missed information. Check any answers you don't fully understand. Ask if there is anything they want to add.

Though you want to avoid any further impositions on the interviewee's time, ensure you have full contact details before you leave the interview. Telephone numbers for work and home, a mobile number, email address and fax number can be lifesavers. Don't hesitate to check facts if you are unsure—the interviewee would undoubtedly prefer you impose on their time, rather than see mistakes printed in the newspaper the next day.

> **TIP:**
> In Step 15 make sure you have answers to the five Ws and one H. If it helps, list these six essential questions in your notepad so it is easy to check at the end (see below).

Who: Jon Coyne, Title: Bank Audit Manager, Bankco
What: Full audit of bank branches
When: At the start of the new financial year
Where: Regional branches
Why: To assess the viability of the branches . . .
How: A full audit incorporating staff, services . . .

Thank the interviewee for their valuable time.

CASE STUDY 2—Soft news feature interview for a personality piece—fifteen key steps

The Bank Audit Manager for Bankco, Jon Coyne, is about to retire after 40 years of service with the same bank. While the first seven steps for a feature interview are relatively similar to those for a news interview, you are seeking different information. As Len Granato notes in *Newspaper Feature Writing*: 'a human-interest feature story is a creative, sometimes subjective, article designed primarily to entertain and only secondarily to inform . . . they are anchored in the human emotions—joy, tragedy, humour, love, hate, sorrow, jealousy' (1997: 3). You will generally have more time in a feature interview to elicit information that should include facts, quotes, anecdotes and description.

Please note that every interview is different and should be treated as such. The following fifteen steps are suggestions for what may be covered in a print feature interview. However Steps 3, 4, 5, 6 and 7 are almost identical in every interview. They have been included here as a reminder.

1. Arrange a couple of interview times
2. Do your research
3. Organise your questions/keywords
4. Organise your notepad and equipment
5. Arrive at the interview early
6. Get set up and check your equipment again
7. Ask your icebreaker question
8. Observe your interviewee and their surroundings
9. Ask your first interview question
10. Don't forget to listen
11. Ask the 'easy' questions first
12. Look for off-beat questions
13. Make time to get anecdotes
14. Gather essential background
15. Check your notes

Fifteen key steps in detail

1. Arrange a couple of interview times. The ideal when interviewing someone for a feature story is to be able to interview them at least twice—preferably face-to-face both times and in different locations. A feature story should cover the public and private persona of the interviewee, and the separate locations can aid in this endeavour. If the story is primarily about their work/hobby/art/sport, the first interview should be conducted where they are involved in these pursuits. In this way you can get a feel for their 'job', their surrounds, and how they interact with others. It would be ideal to catch the person at home for the second interview, but if this is not possible, try and interview them in a 'neutral' location, such as a not-too-noisy café. Confirm any arrangements. Obviously you will need to explain the reason you require the interview/s and where and when it is likely to be published. As with your hard news story, don't give cast-iron guarantees.

2. Do your research. It would be very rare not to have advance notice of print feature interviews. With some celebrities and sports stars you will probably have to organise the interview months in advance. This is good! Use this time to dig hard for everything you can about the interviewee. Celebrities and sport stars tend to get a little jaded because of the number of interviews they conduct, so it is nice if you can surprise them with a new question or information about an interest of theirs which is not widely known. Use primary and secondary sources for your information. Primary sources are other people who can give you reliable information about your interviewee and can include their friends, family, colleagues, team members and employees. Make sure you talk to other primary sources before you do your main interviews. Sometimes your own family, friends and colleagues may also be good sources of information about your interviewee. Secondary sources consist of information produced by others—newspaper clippings, magazine articles, internet sites, journals, books and newsletters are just some.

3. Organise your questions/keywords. Because a feature story will generally be far longer than a news story, you will need to collect more information in your interview/s. This means longer interviews if you have a number of questions and key areas to cover. Even though this is not a news story, it is still helpful to summarise the expected angle or theme before organising the questions/keywords. Write this down in less than 30 words, but don't be concerned if the theme changes after the interview/s.

The following three steps are the same as those used in the news interview.

4. Organise your notepad and equipment.

5. Arrive at the interview early.

6. Get set up and check your equipment again.

7. Ask your icebreaker question. Your research will probably be essential in providing an icebreaker, but don't discount using additional on-the-spot observations to help establish a rapport. For instance, if you are interviewing someone at their home, your observations will be extremely useful to get the conversation going. Photographs, pets, books, trophies and their music collection are obvious clues.

8. Observe your interviewee and their surroundings. Your observations—of both your interviewee and their surroundings—should provide valuable additions to your final story. Feature stories should consist of three main elements: facts, quotes and anecdotes. However many feature writers believe a fourth element—description—should be included as an essential. Len Granato points out that:

> just as people have individual ways of speaking, they have individual ways of looking and acting. They assert their individuality by how they dress, how they wear their hair . . . how they relate to other people, how they feel about things, how they furnish and decorate their personal space. Good description conveys people's images and their personalities (1997: 81).

However, Granato goes on to warn that you 'should never try to tell the reader what to think about anything. Your job is not to instruct the reader but to provide observations that allow the reader to make his or her own interpretations and draw his or her own conclusions' (1997: 81). The interviewee's surroundings should also be included, whether it is at a home, office, studio or favourite coffee shop. Granato points out that you need to 'be selective. Since you can't describe everything, select aspects that will tell the reader something about the source: the photographs of the spouse on the desk, the ship in a bottle on the bookcase, the best actress award on the piano' (1997: 82).

9. Ask your first interview question. With feature interviews it does not hurt to confirm the correct title and spelling of the interviewee's name first. Remember: don't assume anything. As with the news interview, please don't ask for the spelling of the person's name, or their title, if they are well known.

10. Don't forget to listen. It should be understood that listening, and observing, is essential in any interview. Of all the techniques a journalist can use, most agree that listening is the key to interviewing success.

11. Ask the 'easy' questions first. In the case of the feature interview this will depend to a large extent on your interviewee. If it is someone familiar with being interviewed, spend less time at this stage. However, others may be put at ease by a slower start. You will need fact for your story, so collect that first. Questions for Jon Coyne could include: 'Where were you born?' 'Where did you grow up?' 'What was your first job?' 'What is your job now?' 'What are your hobbies?' 'How many children do you have?' 'How many grandchildren do you have?' and so on.

12. Look for off-beat questions. You don't want to overload your story with quotes but you do want to feature some of the interviewee's thoughts and opinions. Jon Coyne could be asked: 'Did you always enjoy your work?' 'Have you had time to enjoy your hobbies/family?' 'What do you think about the banking system of today?' Former newspaper journalist and now interviewer for the ABC Kerry O'Brien says you should be looking for the off-beat questions.

These are the questions that are going to give people that little extra insight into the person you're interviewing that they might not otherwise get, or that

First these in the research.

they won't get if you just ask the predictable. Always be looking for those questions that other journalists are not going to think of (personal interview with Kerry O'Brien, November 2000).

For instance, you could ask Jon Coyne: Did you dream of being a fireman when you were a child?

13. Make time to get anecdotes. Anecdotes are the lifeblood of a feature story. They are basically small stories explaining a situation—usually humorous. They give a story vitality, but are quite difficult to elicit. As you are collecting your facts and quotes, there will invariably be opportunities to ask for anecdotes. Don't be too general when asking for these 'stories'. For instance, asking 'What was the best moment of your career?' is a little general and may prove difficult for the interviewee. However when talking to Jon Coyne about his first job, you may well ask, 'What was your first day like. What was the worst moment/best moment?' When talking about his family, Jon may well tell you that he followed his father's footsteps into banking. He may well have a memory of going in and watching his father at work that would make a great anecdote. This step may take quite a while, and may happen progressively throughout the interview when you are talking about certain topics. You may also elicit anecdotes about your subject from other primary sources such as family and friends.

14. Gather essential background. You will need to find out more about key people in Jon's life, for instance his father, and his wife. This is also the time to get background on the organisation Jon is leaving if this hasn't come up earlier in the interview.

15. Check your notes. With a feature interview you sometimes get the most interesting information at the end when the interviewee relaxes. Check your notes and ask for clarification on any unclear information. You may also have to ask extra questions to elicit anecdotes if you feel you haven't got enough 'colour' in the story. Ask if Jon has anything to add that hasn't been covered. Ensure you have contact details for any follow-up questions.

Don't forget to thank the interviewee for all their valuable time.

REFERENCES

Biagi, S. 1986, *Interviews that Work: A Practical Guide for Journalists*, Wadsworth Publishing Company, Belmont California

Granato, L. 1997, *Newspaper Feature Writing*, Deakin University Press, Geelong

Personal interview with Andrea Carson, October 2000

Personal interview with Kerry O'Brien, November 2000

7

BROADCAST INTERVIEWS

If you want to learn how to interview go and talk to a bunch of kids, because kids give you honest answers and they teach you the most fundamental lesson in radio interviewing and that is—never ask a question to which the answer is 'yes' or 'no' (personal interview with Al Morrison, August 2000).

Radio New Zealand's political editor Al Morrison has been a working journalist all his life and has moved from print journalism to broadcast journalism. So what's the difference? He says that broadcast interviewing is both different from, and the same as, print interviewing. In many ways the same principles of basic, quality journalism apply in broadcast interviewing— asking the right questions, listening and thinking about what it is the public wants to know. But there are differences too. The big difference he says is that 'what you're really aiming for in broadcast interviews is tape'. In television interviews the difference is both the pictures and the tape.

Al Morrison, photo courtesy of Radio New Zealand.

Another important difference relating to live formats is that you as the reporter are likely to be seen as well as heard in broadcast interviews. Your questions may be broadcast during a radio interview and you may be seen and heard during television interviews. In print journalism you may get away with the odd witless question because readers seldom see what was asked, they see only the answers in an edited format within the text of the story. In radio and television there is no place for a dumb question because you may be heard and seen asking it.

THE TYRANNY OF TIME

The tyranny of time nags at broadcast journalists. Australian television journalist Kerry O'Brien agrees, and says if you're doing live interviews for television, or live interviews for radio, you've got the tyranny of time—'the tyranny of the clock ticking'.

And it seems to tick awfully fast when you're in a television studio. Which is why when you get to a certain level of interviewing you will find you're confronted by decisions on the run—whether you really should be interjecting at this point, and at what point you go too far in your interjection, and simply having made your point to the audience, move on. These things can be matters of very fine balance (personal interview with Kerry O'Brien, November 2000).

But it is not only the unremitting nature of deadlines that radio and television journalists have to worry about. They often have to try to make stories as timeless as possible. Time, intimacy and intensity are all accentuated in broadcast interviews. Radio reporters have to cope with reading, writing and creating hourly news bulletins, and perhaps even contributing longer pieces to current affairs stories. Different program formats also require stories of different length and style.

There is what Al Morrison describes as an 'intense intimacy' about radio because it is the most natural of all media. People do much of their communication by talking to each other and radio mimics the way we talk. 'A lot of people listen to the radio and they peel the spuds or weed the garden whereas television and newspaper demand more of your attention' (personal interview with Al Morrison, August 2000).

Australian political radio journalist Fran Kelly says you need an acute sense of where the point of an issue is, 'because that's what you need to get to'.

Within every five-minute interview there should be a gem that you're trying to unwrap. You need to be able to identify that. A lot of people can't see what I call the pointy end of a story. You get better at that as you go on. You need to be a quick thinker in a radio interview, which is my field, because you only have five minutes. Somebody might say something from which you can sense a sort of cascade of connections. You need to be able to jump ten points on (in your head) to focus on that. You need to be able to think quickly and translate that thinking into words very quickly. You need to be a good listener . . . If you're distracted, anything could happen in the interview and before you know it your time's run out (quoted in Wilson 2000: 47).

Television is also about immediacy and reporter involvement. Reporters must quickly learn to go to air live in front of the camera and not make a fool of themselves. Kerry O'Brien points out that 'panic gets you nowhere'. He says it can help to 'force yourself to take five minutes out between when you get your assignment, and when you actually have to do it, to go and look out a window and try and collect your thoughts'.

If you do feel a sense of panic, or think 'God, what am I going to do?', then you just remind yourself that it's all going to be over in a short space of time anyway, and at some point in the not too distant future it will have become a dim memory. In the meantime you're just going to get through it with as much dignity as you can muster (personal interview with Kerry O'Brien, November 2000).

Very often the reporter can be the one being interviewed by an anchor or program host, so the journalist must know as much about being an interviewee as being an interviewer. Reporters also need to know about the different sorts of interviews conducted on radio and television and adapt their interviewing styles accordingly. The different types of interview relate to the use of audio tape in radio reporting and audiovisual tape in television journalism. The highly visual nature of television interviewing means that if there are no pictures, there is no story. Broadcast reporters have to be pushy. At press conferences and out on location they need their microphones and cameras to be well positioned so they can collect good-quality audio tape and visuals.

TAPE

Tape is the most important four-letter word in radio journalism while film is the most important in television. Al Morrison says that in radio interviews 'while you're interviewing you not only have to listen to the content of the answer, you have to listen to it for the 10-, 15-, 30-second or even minute section that really encapsulates what the person is trying to say, not just the dramatic bit but the bit that fairly captures what the person is trying to say' (personal interview with Al Morrison, August 2000). This section or 'grab' can sometimes be as short as 3 to 5 seconds in a radio news bulletin.

Tape comes in different types. Short snips of audio tape are played in a story as part of the broadcast item. These cuts or 'grabs' are usually of people talking, although when New Zealand's Mt Ruapehu volcano erupted, audio tape of the noise of the eruption with rocks, steam and lava belching out of the volcano lake was broadcast. There are four categories of tape: actualities, Q and As, voicers and wraps.

ACTUALITIES

During the Fijian coup in 2000, radio reporters provided tape of people who were actual newsmakers such as the Indian shop-keepers whose stores had been looted and then set on fire. Actualities are basic kinds of tape and allow listeners a chance to hear voices of real people, such as eyewitnesses, who talk naturally and convey the excitement, fear or sadness, and sense of being there. Very often they do not speak grammatically, may use colloquial language and not finish their sentences. Once you have collected the tape from an eyewitness to an event like looting, how do you select the actuality you want? Mitchell Stephens provides the answer in his book on *Broadcast News*:'What sort of comment does a reporter look for in an actuality? Something the newsmaker can say better than the reporter' (1986: 144). Actualities can include eyewitness reports, expert knowledge from the Fijian police, for example, commenting on law and order in the coup, and subjective comments from news sources about their feelings and beliefs.

QUESTION AND ANSWERS

Q and As are where the question is either heard on tape in radio or seen being asked and heard on television. Radio and television interviews that feature questions and answers can be conducted in the studio live. Other broadcast interviews are conducted on the telephone, or at a press conference with other reporters present, as well as face-to-face with a newsmaker. Elite NZ radio and television programs such as 'Holmes' and 'Face the Nation' feature Q and As with reporters such as Paul Holmes and Linda Clark in studio contexts, and radio reporters Geoff Robinson and Sean Plunkett for New Zealand's 'Morning Report' interviewing by question and answer often by telephone hook-up. In Australia, Channel 10's 'Meet the Press' relies solely on the Q and A, while ABC's 'The 7.30 Report' and 'Four Corners', and Channel 9's 'Sunday' program also use this format regularly within their programs.

VOICERS

As elite rugby union player Jonah Lomu was scoring one of his tries against England in the 1995 World Cup, veteran New Zealand rugby commentator Keith Quinn lost his notes.

Quinn was forced to do a 'voicer', a reporter's monologue, interviewing himself before retreating to his notes again. Quinn lost the comfort of prepared statistics and sports commentary superlatives that had been scripted beforehand and had to improvise into the microphone. Many voicers are, in fact, written out in advance but usually on the run—on a scrap of paper, in a field notepad, or an address book—or in the car. Voicers are sometimes referred to in television as part of the 'stand-up syndrome' by which reporters stand in front of the camera and become the newsmaker and can be an alternative when there is no newsmaker present such as describing a fire or Mt Ruapehu erupting before officials or survivors can be found for interviews. They can supplement Q and As and actualities.

WRAPS

Wraps are like a broadcast sandwich, with one layer of a voicer then a layer of actuality and then a voicer again. First the reporter's voice is heard, then the newsmaker is heard with the reporter heard again in conclusion.

The reporter wraps the story around the actuality and usually it becomes a self-contained story. For example:

Reporter: Mt Ruapehu erupted again yesterday belching smoke, rocks and lava several kilometres into the sky. Hot lava flows threaten to engulf ski fields, the famous Chateau tourist hotel and the township of Ohakune. Residents and shopkeepers are preparing to evacuate and most like Mayor Sarah Dogood agree they have little choice but to leave their homes.

Newsmaker: There is no way we can risk the safety of our kids and our families by staying put. If we lose everything we may be financially ruined but at least we'll be alive.

Reporter:	Chief vulcanologist Joe Blow says he expects Mt Ruapehu to continue erupting for several days and he warns of new fissures in the crater lake.

NATURAL SOUND

A reporter covering the Mt Ruapehu eruption recorded reaction to the natural phenomenon in a local pub. But back in the newsroom her actualities missed a vital element. She was sent back to the mountain to get the rumble, hiss and roar of the mountain erupting as background noise. Make sure you capture quality natural sound to edit into stories. Sound effects are important for authenticity and interest in radio news and add to the dramatic effect of visuals in television news.

TIPS FOR BROADCAST INTERVIEWING

These tips have been compiled after talking with experienced broadcast journalists about the dos and don'ts of broadcast interviews.

1. Listen, listen and listen

The most important advice for anyone conducting a broadcast interview is to actively listen to what the interviewee is saying. Interviewing is primarily a listening exercise. In broadcast interviewing you often only get one chance—particularly if the interview is live.

Top New Zealand radio and television interviewer Dr Brian Edwards believes you need to put aside your prepared interview structure in favour of following a listening lead:

If somebody hangs a bait in front of you and it's a good piece of bait you've got to take it. If you are not listening you're going to miss it and that will frustrate your listener or viewer. So when somebody says, 'Yes, I did go to university, this was just after I murdered my second wife' and you say 'What subjects did you do at university?', the listeners and viewers know you're not listening. A good interviewer is constantly monitoring what's going on (personal interview with Dr Brian Edwards, October 2000).

2. Establish rapport

Forming some sort of rapport with the person to be interviewed before the interview is absolutely critical to what happens at the interview. Dr Edwards says:

A lot of young interviewers both in news and current affairs and in the more personality-driven interviews walk in and say, 'Hi, my name is Jeanette and can you come through to the studio'. They will ask the first question in such a way that the interviewee goes in absolutely cold, has no sense of relationship with the interviewer and takes a long time to warm up and may not warm up at all. You must form a rapport and that involves developing certain intuitive skills (personal interview with Dr Brian Edwards, October 2000).

3. Avoid 'yes' and 'no' answers

Do not ask the bad broadcast question which results in a 'yes' or 'no' answer such as: 'I understand you saw the mountain erupt?' Questions should be phrased so that the person being interviewed does the talking. For example, 'What did you see when Mt Ruapehu erupted?'

Do ask questions that stimulate conversation and prompt questions that will interest your audience. 'What', 'How' and 'Why' questions are often useful starting points. 'How would you describe . . .', and 'How would you explain the background . . .' are other invitations to newsmakers to do the talking.

4. Be kind to amateurs

Some newsmakers are 'oncers'. They are in the right place at the wrong time or the wrong place at the right time and witness tragedy, accidents, war, natural disasters or unique events. Amateur newsmakers have little knowledge or understanding of the intricacies of broadcast interviews and aren't used to dealing with the media. Good broadcast journalists make a distinction between those who know how to use the media and those who don't. You need to be kinder as an interviewer to those with no experience of the news media. Radio New Zealand's political editor, Al Morrison, says:

> With politicians an interview which has a degree of entrapment, draws them to a point, and then whams them with a question out of the blue is legitimate. It isn't if you are talking to someone who isn't media savvy and who you couldn't expect to be, like someone at an accident site (personal interview with Al Morrison, August 2000).

This might only be fair if we can logically expect that they should know the answer & that it is info applicable to the interview.

At the other end of the scale some public figures are so adept at interviews that you can ask them for a 10-second 'grab' on a particular issue or event, and that's precisely what you'll get.

5. Guide the interview

In a media-centric world victims should, on cue, say that their plight is terrible, victorious sport winners should be ecstatic and gracious about their opposition in equal measure, and those who survive death-defying accidents should talk of miracle escapes. While these reactions are the ones journalists pray for, news sources are not always so obliging. You know what you want as a reporter on tape from the people you interview. So how far can you go?

Most broadcast reporters believe that guiding is appropriate so that those making the news say the right things and provide usable tape. But it is inappropriate to coach people you interview or put words in their mouths. Al Morrison agrees:

You often have to repeat questions and sometimes you actually have to stop midstream and do a little training and say 'Look, I'm not trying to put words into your mouth but what you're saying to me that's interesting is this and this and this . . . do you think you could put those three things together in one statement' . . . there's an element of training to that which I don't have a problem with because talking into a tape recorder or a microphone is not something that people naturally do (personal interview with Al Morrison, August 2000).

6. Keep on track

Newsmakers can quickly go down a different track during an interview. You have to keep the interview focused on what it is the public wants to know. Sometimes it is the answer to one question only.

If you ask a question and somebody sort of strolls off and leads you on to asking a couple more questions about another subject which may well be interesting, that's fine, but come back again. Always come back again. Even if it requires making a note in front of yourself saying 'Ask that question' (Kim Hill 1996).

Kerry O'Brien (who won the 2000 Walkley Award for Best Interviewing) says he doesn't have particular tricks in the way he does interviews.

I simply endeavour to understand as much as I can by way of background reading on the subject, and try to focus in on its essential elements. What are the things that the public would really want to know about this, which are the most interesting and compelling aspects? What is the time that I have available? How much can I realistically hope to fit into that time? And I then order the questions accordingly (personal interview with Kerry O'Brien, November 2000).

GETTING THE GRAB: THE HARD NEWS INTERVIEW

The key to getting the grab is timing and the right question. In hard news interviews the questions are likely to be closed questions, questions that are quite specific and which are intended to restrict the focus of the answer to the question. In an interview about euthanasia on Radio New Zealand, Kim Hill followed up a television story about a tetraplegic who had broken his neck in two places in a truck accident. The tetraplegic could not move his limbs, could not breathe without a ventilator and had written to the health authority requesting the right to end his life. Twelve days had elapsed between the time he was filmed about his euthanasia request and the story's broadcast, during which time the patient felt more positive. Kim Hill wanted to explore the issue of a patient's change of mind about euthanasia with a hospice medical director. After setting the scene Kim asked a series of focused, closed questions in a hard news interview conducted live.

The questions were direct. She asked whether it mattered that television had filmed the patient twelve days before screening the program and in that time the tetraplegic may have undergone a slight change of mind. She also challenged the interviewee about the logic of patients assessing their lives and deciding that living a poor quality of life was not something they wanted. In the course of the interview she very directly asked the medical director if during the time he had worked at the hospice he had changed his mind about euthanasia. The medical director replied that yes, when he first went into hospice work 'I was right down the end of the spectrum that said euthanasia is bad and we must not even consider it'. Since then numbers of people had spoken to him about the wretched state of their lives and he felt more empathy and understanding with them. 'But I think that I still haven't changed,' he said.

During the hard news interview Kim Hill set the scene, introduced her interview guest, asked short closed questions that focused the interviewee, listened to the replies and followed up leads, asked the interviewee the right questions and then asked the tough question that forced the interviewee to reveal his feelings about the purpose of life and euthanasia. While the sensitivity of the subject was acknowledged, the relevant, 'hard' questions were asked and radio listeners felt they had been part of a purposeful conversation. That is the essence of a hard news broadcast interview.

THE SOFT NEWS INTERVIEW

Soft news interviews on radio and television have one thing in common. They are extended conversations with people telling stories and they employ open questions. Dr Brian Edwards says the extended broadcast interview probably has only one question: 'Tell me about it, tell me your story . . . in a nutshell you are looking for stories. Stories, stories, stories. Examples, illustrations, people want to hear stories . . . that's what makes an extended interview work' (personal interview with Dr Brian Edwards, October 2000).

As the master of thousands of soft broadcast news interviews Dr Edwards offers the following tips.

Chase away butterflies

Helping interviewees overcome nerves is essential so that they perform well. You must recognise how nervous many people are at being interviewed for radio and television even if the interview is an extended, soft interview and even if they are experienced.

If what you're looking for is a successful newsy conversation where both parties are at ease then maybe a bit of flattery up at the front of the interview does not do any harm. Most of my intros to people I was interviewing on radio on Saturday morning were actually very flattering. You looked across the table and you could see the interviewee melt a little and lose some of their nervousness because they think that 'this fellow had a bit of a reputation as a hard-liner' but this isn't going to be like that.

As well as flattery, try reassurance and self-disclosure along the lines of, 'Look, I'm sure you're feeling a bit nervous, I'm getting a bit nervous myself'. Relaxed interviewees will be more candid, reveal more of themselves and enjoy the interview experience.

Don't irritate the interviewee before the start

A common failing of inexperienced interviewers is that they irritate or annoy the interviewee before the interview has started. Displays of indifference and discourtesy to the news-maker in the studio can be offputting. Chatting to someone in a civilised and interested manner before the interview is a way of establishing mutual respect even if hard questions have to be asked later.

You don't realise it but people expect a degree of respect and may feel that they've put themselves out a bit to be there and do the interview. They don't want to be treated like a disposable piece of meat. Once you get into interview mode you may have to turn the knife a little but don't go out and be hostile before you start.

Think about the opening question

An extended interview has a rhythm of its own and listeners and viewers need to feel that the interview went somewhere. Interview structure is important so that the conversation has a satisfying form to it. A soft interview needs an introduction, development of the material, a conclusion of some sort, with some light and heavier exchanges in between. The opening question sets the scene.

I'm a great admirer of John Hurt the actor and was looking forward to doing an interview with him. I met him for about 5 or 6 minutes just before the interview and he looked really hung over. In addition to being really hung over he was chain smoking. As an interviewer you will often pick up on little, seemingly inconsequential things as an entrée to the interview. They may be little things you have noticed or things someone has told you. An interviewee will be chatting to you while a record is playing and they'll mention a reminiscence of something about themselves. That's often a very valuable way of forming early rapport. So we chatted for a moment or two about his smoking and then when I started the interview I began by asking him about his smoking in a totally disapproving way. 'Why are you smoking cigarettes? . . . Don't you know it's bad for you.' It rocked the interview and took me 20 minutes to get back on track, so that was really bad judgement.

Watch your time

There is a danger of loss of control in the soft news interview and as the interviewer you have to exercise time judgement. Ask yourself, 'How much time can I afford to spend on this subject?' If you spend too much time on a tangential subject you risk missing the core topic that might be further down the track.

Dr Brian Edwards, photo courtesy of Dr Edwards.

Open questions can be hazardous. There is a risk that the interviewee will wander off down some track so you're always a ringmaster in an interview and you're always controlling it, keeping it on track and bringing people back to the point. I did an appalling interview with the wife of a great pioneer film maker where I spent a whole lot of time talking to her about her background and almost never got around to the movie-making. That was a terrible mistake.

Keep eye contact

During the interview it pays to keep up a non-verbal dialogue with the interviewee which helps them relax, be spontaneous and enter into the spirit of the conversation.

Eye contact with your interviewee is terribly important. You never take your eyes off the person. You treat them like a lover so they lose all sense of everything around them. Women say they find men who pay them attention attractive. It is the same with interviews. You pay the interviewee a lot of attention.

Involve the interviewee in the dynamics of the interview

Novice interviewers often bury their heads in their notes the whole time. Interviewers do have to refer to written material or question sheets during an extended interview to refresh themselves about a line of questioning. But involve your interviewee in the interview process. Tell them about the studio and the procedures.

I will often say to an interviewee that I'll be looking down a bit because I've got my questions on my sheet but please don't think that I am not interested in what you're saying. Tell them what the game is all about.

Be wary of clippings

Research is essential for extended interviews. Often soft interviews are conducted with personalities and celebrities, visiting stars and sports people who have been written about comprehensively. These clippings form part of the celebrity archaeology that all broadcast interviewers undertake in the research process. But be wary.

> A danger of clippings, of course, is that they may not be accurate. You could find yourself saying to a studio guest 'You did this and that' and the person responding 'No, I bloody did not' and 'Who told you that?' and then you're in trouble. Cuttings that come from the tabloid press or women's magazines can be dangerous. On the other hand something you found in the *Women's Weekly* 20 years ago might make a brilliant line of questioning.

Try for a good end

Just as an interview needs a good opening to grab listener and viewer attention it also needs a good end to be memorable. You want to try to finish well and it is important in long interviews to have an end in mind. Former New Zealand Prime Minister Robert Muldoon would note the wind-up cues in live, television studio interviews and turn abruptly to the camera and commandeer the last seconds with a direct message to his own advantage. As an interviewer you need to be in control of the interview and ensure that you, rather than your guest, end the interview. Beware, too, the interview that dribbles to an end. You will have lost the audience.

HORROR BROADCAST INTERVIEWS

All broadcasters can remember interviews they'd prefer to forget. Sometimes the interview is a disaster because the equipment fails, you forget to turn on the microphone, the batteries in the tape recorder fail or the film is unusable for technical reasons. In these cases the interview may not get to air. In other cases horror interviews occur not for technical reasons but because you get off on the wrong foot with an interviewee, you ask a question the interviewee objects to or you persist with a line of questioning that doesn't work. Because you're on-air or in a studio with live audiences these can be nerve-racking experiences for the interviewer, the newsmaker and the audience. Dr Brian Edwards recalls a disaster of an interview with American jazz great Duke Ellington.

> I had a question which had come up in the research which was along the lines of 'There seems to be no evidence of you having done anything to really support the struggle of black people in the United States'. He was immediately infuriated by the question and turned to me at the interview and said, 'This interviewing business isn't your bag'. Afterwards I realised that his contribution to the black movement of the United States was his music and not standing up and making speeches. It was a really misjudged question and it was not meant to be that sort of interview (personal interview with Dr Brian Edwards, October 2000).

Freezing and 'umms' and 'ahhs'

As well as technical troubles and bad judgement calls by the broadcaster, interviews can be fraught when either the newsmaker or the reporter freezes. Radio New Zealand's political editor Al Morrison says the really horrific broadcast interviews are the ones in which people freeze into silence. He recalls a radio station crossing to a reporter for a live account of a parliamentary protest demonstration. The reporter froze and couldn't speak. Back in the studio the silence had to be filled with improvised talk while other linkages were made. When amateur newsmakers, who are not accustomed to being in the news, freeze in front of the microphones or cameras it is often because of the unnatural intrusion of the technical equipment. They suddenly realise that the world is watching and listening to them and they become nervous. It pays to try to minimise technological intrusion in certain sorts of broadcast interviews.

'Umming' and 'ahhing', mumbling and poor enunciation and pronunciation turn off the audience in broadcast interviews. They are very obvious when reporters are doing pieces to camera. Breathing exercises before facing the camera and going on air, thinking about the question and not your answer, slowing your speech down, consciously trying to avoid 'umms' are all techniques used by broadcast journalists to avoid the verbal fumbles. Al Morrison says he's very aware of his voice as a radio broadcaster. While he walks into work he does voice exercises, stretching his vocal chords, talking to himself out loud and thinking about the art of performance as a broadcast journalist.

VIDEOJOURNALISM

Some journalists in smaller television stations today have added pressures resulting from modern technology and staff cuts. These 'videojournalists' not only have to conduct their own interviews, but also get video footage of the interview and sometimes even edit the piece. Videojournalists need to be flexible, multiskilled, and gather and produce quality stories. Armed with a digital camera and tripod these videojournalists must ensure that they obtain good footage and sound, as well as strong 'grabs'. There are several advantages of being a 'one person team'. In an Australian newspaper article entitled 'Low-cost quality' it is noted that 'Video-journalism has come of age when reporters on a program of the stature of "Dateline" (SBS) are heralded at Australian journalism's premier awards night for work they reported, produced, directed, filmed, and at least partly edited'. 'Dateline' journalist Mark Davis describes it as a 'humanistic approach to news' where the reporter has to 'think about the people rather than the story'. 'It's more intimate,' he says. 'People will invite one person to stay, or ride in their car, which they wouldn't do with a three or four person crew.' There's also a huge cost advantage, not just in crew costs or cheaper cameras, but in things like travelling on a bus rather than a hire car. ' "It's a real advantage with this stuff that people are off your back about cost" says Davis' (Plane 2000: 'Media' 14).

REFERENCES:

Hill, K. 1996, *Advanced Interviewing Skills for Journalists*, National Diploma in Journalism, Wellington Polytechnic and the Open Polytechnic of NZ quoted with permission from the broadcaster

Personal interview with Dr Brian Edwards, October 2000

Personal interview with Al Morrison, August 2000

Personal interview with Kerry O'Brien, November 2000

Plane, T. 2000, 'Low-cost quality', *The Australian*, 14–20 December 2000, 'Media' p. 14

Stephens, M. 1986, *Broadcast News*, 2nd edn, CBS College Publishing, New York

Wilson, R. 2000, *A Big Ask: Interviews with Interviewers*, New Holland Publishers, Sydney

8 TELEPHONE AND EMAIL INTERVIEWS

> One newspaper editor was known to call cadets into his office, pull the phone out of the wall connection and throw it across the room to show his displeasure at its over-use. A bit dramatic perhaps, but it certainly got the point across!

While the face-to-face interview is the ideal way of gathering information from primary sources, it is steadily becoming a less common method used by journalists. Today more interviews are being conducted by fewer staff who are turning to faster methods of news gathering. The two most common time-saving methods used today are telephone and email interviews. While they do not have the advantage of providing non-verbal cues (such as eye contact and body language), they are very convenient for both the interviewer and interviewee. This is particularly the case with email interviews where those involved in the exchange are in different time zones. Australian journalism educator and author Barbara Alysen says the advantage of telephone interviews can be summed up as: 'A reporter who doesn't have to leave the office is a reporter who can squeeze more stories into a working day'. However, she agrees the 'downside is that the interviewer can't use the normal methods of establishing rapport such as eye contact and body language' (2000: 131).

Newspaper editors tend to frown on the use (or over-use) of the telephone interview, while broadcast news editors generally accept it as a necessity imposed by tight deadlines. The former believe journalists should be out and about talking to people and looking for stories on a continual basis—not waiting for the phone to ring, or using the phone to contact people for local rounds. While a high percentage of face-to-face interviews may be possible for print journalists, radio journalists producing five news bulletins or more each day have little choice but to rely heavily on the phone to interview sources and record sound bites.

Most journalists go to great lengths to avoid the telephone interview—preferring the face-to-face exchange. However telephone interviews do provide some important clues including tone of voice, silence, volume and laughter. It is essential, too, that the journalist provides encouragement for the interviewee when conducting an interview on the telephone.

One cadet who always spent extra time talking to police sergeants, ambulance officers and other daily contacts was often rewarded with front page stories. She tells the tale of chatting away about a local football match one day when the police sergeant interrupted with: 'You haven't heard, have you?' 'About?' she asked. 'Go down to the wharf right now, and there'll be a story for you,' he replied. The story was a double-murder, and an exclusive page 1 scoop for the reporter.

BEWARE OF THE AVOIDANCE FACTOR

While email and telephone interviews are convenient for reporters, they can be equally convenient for elusive news sources. Politicians, sports stars, public officials and celebrities sometimes don't want to reply to email inquiries. Some also have gatekeepers fobbing off phone calls. There is also a raft of telephone paging devices and mobile phones that incorporate technology allowing the receiver to know who is calling before answering. This permits avoidance behaviour. Reliance on email or telephone interviewing is probably a mistake if the news source wants to play hard to get. Only persistent and ingenious methods of making contact with elusive news sources works.

Both telephone and email interviews have a certain protocol, and steps that should be taken to increase the success of the exchange. Twelve essential steps for conducting telephone and email interviews, with explanations and advice for each step, are provided below. However, in any exchange, whether face-to-face or via a telephone or computer terminal, politeness and curiosity are still essentials.

THE TELEPHONE INTERVIEW

1. The first step for any telephone interview should be to introduce your organisation, yourself, and the fact that you want to do an interview for publication—print or broadcast. Put your name second, as people sometimes miss the first few words of a phone conversation. You should quickly follow this introduction by asking the interviewee if they have a few minutes to spare. If they don't, respect this, and ask when you might be able to call again to interview them. If they do indicate they have the time, repeat the details about the interview, what information you would like from them, and where and when it might be used. If you can avoid it, try not to pressure people into giving you detailed information in a hurry. This may not always be possible, particularly for radio journalists, but most people will not appreciate being given a

tight deadline, and may either refuse to be interviewed or be abrupt in their responses.

2. Thank anyone who takes the trouble to return your messages—it doesn't happen that often!

3. As a general rule smile while you are talking on the phone. Try it, and you will realise that it makes you sound much more encouraging and friendly. However, you may not want to do this in every telephone interview, particularly if you are asking 'tough' questions. Don't talk too loudly or softly, just use your ordinary speaking voice. If you're using a mobile phone, make sure you're in an area where the signal is strong and won't drop out.

4. Restrict your icebreaker. As a general rule you are using the telephone as a time-saver, so get to the interview as quickly as you can.

5. Have your questions or keywords well organised before you get on the line. You don't want to be wasting the other person's time while you are searching through pieces of paper to find your list.

6. Keep your questions simple. This should always be the case, but it is particularly difficult for interviewees to remember long and complex questions on the telephone. Two sentences is the maximum—one sentence is better. Don't be afraid to ask for examples, and even description. The latter is particularly important if you are conducting a feature interview over the phone. Journalism educator and author Carole Rich (2000) writes about an American reporter, Nancy Tracy, who had a way of 'almost seeing through the telephone'.

> She would ask her sources for details. She asked what they were wearing, what they were doing, what they were thinking, how they were coping and reacting. An introduction from a feature story she wrote includes this

detail obtained on the phone. 'Some days when the pain isn't too bad, he stands by the front door, watching trucks roll by on Highway 41 on their way to Macon. Then the memories come flooding back, the crash, the pain' (2000: 132).

Some journalists abhor that she got this over the phone.

7. Take down your notes as quickly as possible. If you're recording the interview for broadcast, or for your own record, you must tell the interviewee before you start.

8. Ensure you understand all the answers given. If you don't, ask again, or request a simpler explanation. Don't be afraid to admit you don't understand—you can't be an expert in every field.

9. Listen carefully and be ready to follow up any unexpected answers.

10. Be polite from beginning to end. Keep your cool—even when your interviewee does not.

11. Obtain the correct spelling of the interviewee's name, and their correct title. Repeat these back over the line if you are unsure.

12. Don't forget to obtain contact details. Try not to call people outside work hours—unless unavoidable. Thank the interviewee for their valuable time.

THE EMAIL INTERVIEW

The email interview is an excellent way to contact your sources for information, and far cheaper than using the telephone. Contacting people quickly and cheaply anywhere on the globe is the major advantage, though your emails can easily be ignored. These interviews can either be conducted in 'real time', with both the interviewer and interviewee logged on at the same time, or can be sent and delivered as ordinary emails with the interviewee replying in their own time.

Author Jane Dorner says 'Email interviewing doesn't replace intuitively following your subject's lead and getting clues from tone of voice, but telephone interviewing was itself always a poor second to the face-to-face chat' (2000: 32). Rich agrees, noting that 'Although it is not preferable to interviewing by telephone or in person, email is an option for interviewing sources who can't be reached otherwise or can't spare time for other forms of contact' (2000: 102–3). Andrea Carson, industrial reporter with Melbourne's *Age*, says she uses email more for establishing and maintaining contacts, rather than for interviews. She believes there's no pressure on the recipient to answer the questions, and in her role as industrial reporter the questions are often tough ones that require this pressure. Andrea says she is more likely to use email for introducing herself to new and potential contacts, and after she has established the contact, for maintaining communication.

Reporter Richard Trow uses email interviewing in his job as defence reporter for *The Dominion*, and as a former reporter for the New Zealand paper's 'Infotech Weekly' section.

> I started to use email interviews particularly for offshore interviews and to overcome time differences around the world. I found that they were very useful for background interviews and for conducting friendly interviews and engaging people in factual debate. I very quickly came to the conclusion, though, that there were difficulties with email interviews if you wanted to ask tough questions (personal interview with Richard Trow, November 2000).

Richard says the reporter gives away too much power to the news source in these email interviews. 'If someone doesn't want to answer, or claims not to be there, you have lost control.' Richard says email interviewing also allows a news source to take material and show it to public relations people before replying. He has two tips for email interviewing:

1. Structure your questions in point form, one by one. If you lump what you want to know together then news sources can leave out questions that are difficult, or ignore questions. Following this advice you would conduct your email interview as: 1. How was the fraud discovered? 2. Why did you leave the company? And so on.

2. Avoid unduly irritating a news source by activating the urgency of your email interview. Richard says it irritates him when he receives 'High urgency' and 'Top priority' emails when they are not, so he recommends you don't use this protocol.

> And DO be careful about assuming the veracity of a news source in an email interview. Someone else could be logged on or sitting at the computer other than the source you think you have quoted accurately. While an email response may be an insurance against misreporting claims because you have a verbatim record, it may be no defence if it wasn't written and sent by the source you thought you were in email conversation with (personal interview with Richard Trow, November 2000).

The following are recommended steps for an email interview.

1. The first step is an introductory one. For the email interview there really is a protocol for organising an interview because you can't determine immediately if the interviewee has time to be involved in an interview. So send an email to your interviewee introducing yourself and your organisation and requesting the interview. Do not include anything

more than an introduction here. Jane Dorner, author of *The Internet: A Writer's Guide*, believes 'Online interviewing is exactly like traditional interviewing. The first email should be exploratory, introducing yourself and your publication. Use the same formality register as you would in any other circumstance; email doesn't give you a licence to be casual' (2000: 33).

2. The next step should be to ensure the interviewee is well aware of the purpose of the interview. Rich notes that you should also clarify your purpose very early and 'make it clear that you intend to use the email message in a news story. Personal email messages are not intended for publication' (2000: 134).

3. If they agree to an interview, decide how it is to be conducted—in 'real time' or in the interviewee's own time. 'Real time' is probably preferable as you can get the information you need immediately, follow up on any answers you don't understand, and ask for clarification and more information as required. It also means the answers are more spontaneous.

4. If you have chosen a 'real time' interview you should start with some sort of summary statement on what you hope to achieve in the interview, and determine how long the interviewee has to 'talk' to you.

5. Ask your first question. Because the questions are available visually (on screen), they can contain far more information than questions asked on the telephone, or during a face-to-face interview. Jane Dorner believes 'using email to interview forces you to be more prepared by formulating questions in advance. It's less intrusive, allowing you to ask your questions at any hour of the day without bothering anyone' (2000: 32). However she cautions that it's best to start with just a few questions. 'A whole barrage of questions in one email is off-putting and will make the subject

feel they are writing the article for you. It's best to bounce to and fro and build up an iterative picture' (2000: 33). The more questions you include, the more you reduce your chance of getting a response.

6. Don't be afraid to ask for clarification, or perhaps an answer worded in a simpler way.

7. Be prepared to follow up unexpected answers, but don't allow the interview to stray too far from the original topic.

8. Determine how long you are prepared to wait for an answer. If you haven't heard from the interviewee after a couple of minutes (allowing time for formulating and typing an answer and then sending it), you may want to send a short note asking if they need the question reworded or clarified.

9. Make sure you have your questions/keywords in front of you, and check these to make sure you have covered them all before concluding the interview.

10. Check the spelling of the interviewee's name and their correct title. Often an abbreviated version is used in emails and sometimes a nickname is used. Always confirm these details.

11. Ensure you have contact times, numbers and addresses before signing off.

12. Thank the interviewee for their valuable time. Print out the full exchange immediately, and don't forget to contact them again when the article comes out.

One of the major advantages of an email interview is that you have a written record of the questions and answers—so you can't be accused of misquoting. The major disadvantage, particularly with an exchange conducted over a period of time (not 'real time'), is that the answers are not spontaneous and may lack 'colour'. As Jane Dorner points out, the 'email interview gives your subject time to think, so chances are that they

Not in the U.S.!!

Confused? Admit it. Confirmed

will express what they really want to say more carefully. You can always email back an amended version of the quote if need be and get a quick "agreed" in return' (2000: 32).

As email interviews are in written form, you must ensure that your questions are well framed and not vague. You are also relying heavily on the fact that your interviewee will be 'good talent'. However be prepared for the fact that you may be interviewing someone who is not conversant with email, has difficulty formulating written answers (though they may be extremely articulate on the phone or in person), and who may use streams of bureaucratic jargon. Your interviewee may also be a 'two-finger typist', so responses may be a long time coming.

Email interviews have also been broadcast during television programs, when the source was hesitant to appear in person. It was appropriately used during a current affairs program about the Internet entitled 'Domain Games' (ABC, 5 June 2000). The reporter, Stephen McDonell, interviewed Australian Internet pioneer Robert Elz for ABC's 'Four Corners', and the answers were projected on a computer screen just as they would have appeared during an email interview. Below is an excerpt from the interview.

> Stephen McDonell: The elusive Mr Elz did, however, talk to us about the Hawaiian link using a medium with which he feels comfortable—email.
>
> . . .
>
> Robert Elz: That was the beginning of true Internet connectivity.
> It meant better communications—more facilities.
> It meant that Australia was as good as the rest of the world, I suppose.
> It also provided the impetus to get the universities to build AARNet—the original Internet segment around Australia. (http://www.abc.net.au/4corners/stories/s136215.htm)

REFERENCES

Alysen, B. 2000, *The Electronic Reporter*, Deakin University Press, Geelong

Dorner, J. 2000, *The Internet: A Writer's Guide*, A. & C. Black, London

Personal interview with Andrea Carson, November 2000

Personal interview with Richard Trow, November 2000

Rich, C. 2000, *Writing and Reporting News: A Coaching Method*, 3rd edn, Wadsworth Publishing Company, Belmont California

http://www.abc.net.au/4corners/stories/s136215.htm

9

USING THE INFORMATION

[handwritten note: Beware: this chapter covers thing's in GB law.]

> 'Well, we knocked the bastard off!' Sir Edmund Hillary on conquering Mt Everest, 1953 (Knowles 1998: 149).

> 'That's one small step for man, one giant leap for mankind.' Neil Armstrong as he walked on the moon (Knowles 1998: 13).

Quotes are the pearls of journalism. We recall brilliant lines by great and ordinary people that have been quoted by journalists. Some quotes are immortalised and become part of our shared culture and history. A former New Zealand Finance Minister, Ruth Richardson, described her 1992 budget as the 'mother of all budgets'. The words 'mother of all' are now commonly attached to any number of products, activities and issues with New Zealanders all knowing the reference point. Similarly, the phrase 'orchestrated litany of lies', coined by the judge who conducted the Mt Erebus plane crash inquiry, has entered the Kiwi vocabulary and is used by editorial writers, politicians and ordinary people when talking about lying. Lines from former

[handwritten note: 1991 – Saddam Hussein "Mother of all wars".]

Australian political leaders, such as Sir Joh Bjelke-Petersen's 'feeding the chooks' (referring to speaking to the media), and Don Chipp's 'keep the bastards honest' (when talking of other political parties), are still frequently used today. Quotes—when to use them and when to avoid them, when to paraphrase and when to use direct speech—are only a few of the judgements that reporters have to make quickly after they have conducted the interview.

Quotes can:

- Bring a living, active feel to a story
- Lend authenticity
- Allow audiences to hear the voices of people in the news
- Provide an accurate summary
- Provide proof of what was said in controversial issues or legal contexts
- Catch provisos, nuances and distinctions in passages of speech
- Provide colour, tone and flavour to a story
- Make the story contemporary with the use of colloquialisms

DO USE direct quotes from an interview when the news source says something better than you can as the reporter. When we were interviewing for this book, veteran New Zealand broadcaster Dr Brian Edwards spoke of how he keeps eye contact with his interviewees. 'You never take your eyes off the person. You treat them like a lover so they lose all sense of everything around them' (personal interview with Dr Brian Edwards, October 2000). A great quote like that should never be paraphrased. Imagine how it would sound or read if you took the words out of direct speech.

DON'T TRY to use direct quotes when the news source is simply reciting factual information or giving you omnibus information. In those pedestrian cases 'it's like trying to set the telephone directory to music' (Cappon 1982: 73). Avoid padding out a story with quotes or simply repeating material with quotes.

> **TIP:**
>
> Before rushing to the computer or telephone to use the information you've gathered in the interview, pause for a minute to
>
> - mark the best quotes,
> - read over all that was said for context, flavour and tone,
> - work out who else needs to be interviewed for a story, and
> - identify the angle.

HOW TO GET GOOD QUOTES

Good quotes should summarize what's on a person's mind, crystallize an emotion or attitude, offer an individual perspective of some sort—preferably in a concise and interesting way (Cappon 1982: 72).

Some sources are living, breathing quote machines. Everything they say is rich in tone and flavour. Others, such as politicians like former New Zealand Prime Minister David Lange, can be guaranteed to drop at least one great line per news conference. Sometimes the best quotes come as brilliant flashes from unlikely people. In other cases good quotes are hard to come by. The news source is wary, wooden or monosyllabic. In these cases you have to work hard in an interview to get good quotes. Here's some tips for extracting the best possible quotes from those you interview:

- Try to relax the news source.
- Establish trust between yourself and the source by using good interpersonal skills and displaying empathy.
- Spend extra time in person with the news source or on the phone, it might yield dividends.
- Actively listen for clues in answers that will lead to a question that flushes out a choice quote.
- Ask quality questions that are more likely to produce quality responses.
- Try the occasional spontaneous but intelligent 'left field' question in soft news interviews.

You should immediately recognise a good quote when it is uttered. Either during the interview or immediately afterwards mark or underline the good quotes so you can angle your story around the best quotes. Use the top quotes from the interview as direct quotes. Paraphrase the factual information or the pedestrian pieces of the interview.

While asking a good question is more likely to produce usable quotes, you need to be careful about including the question in a direct quote. The Australian Press Council draws attention to the undesirability of attributing statements as direct quotes to a person who is responding to a question. The question should not be included in the person's direct quote (Adjudication No. 9 1977).

'I WAS MISQUOTED . . .'

This is the most common complaint to editors and regulatory bodies about reporters. Misquotation is easy to do and painful to rectify. There are different types of complaints about mis-quotation which you should recognise. The following types of complaints are typical:

- complaints from people who are accurately quoted but don't like the reaction to the words quoted,
- complaints from news sources who didn't know they were being quoted,
- complaints from people who were caught off-guard and are now embarrassed,
- complaints from people who are genuinely misquoted, and
- complaints from people who think they should have been quoted and weren't.

Misquotation can occur directly because the words as printed were not a direct quotation or indirectly because of the context in which the quotes are published distorts the meaning. Award-winning Australian journalist Kerry O'Brien says he doesn't believe in the practice of changing the order of answers or changing the actual questions used, as this can 'alter the nuance' and give an unrealistic view of the context in which the statements were made (personal interview with Kerry O'Brien, November 2000).

There is no single rule about what to do when a news source complains about misquotation. If you have taped the interview then you will have evidence about the accuracy of the quotation. Similarly shorthand notes provide a measure of protection. When the complaint is vexatious you should expect support from the newsroom or the publisher of the story.

In cases where you've made a mistake, it pays to put it right as soon as possible. When a Sydney Sunday newspaper wrongly claimed that former Test cricket captain Mark Taylor was set to urge Australians to vote against the 'Yes' case in the consti-tutional referendum under the heading 'Tubby Bats for Queen', the editor went some way to make amends but not far enough. He offered a personal apology to Mark Taylor, he apologised on radio and in letters to readers he said the newspaper only wished to publish stories that were truthful and accurate. The Australian Press Council, however, said the newspaper's 'claimed two million readers were owed a prominent explanation as to how it got the report so wrong' (Adjudication No. 1057 1999).

ARE QUOTES SACRED?

This was the heading in an *American Journalism Review* article discussing whether journalists should ever change quotes. There are usually newsroom rules about whether quotes are to be changed or not. Should someone's comment be made grammatically correct, embellished so it is more colourful, or altered so it is easier to follow? There has always been wide disagreement over the extent to which quotes should be altered. Often, too, it is not the reporter who alters the quote but the next person in the news production chain.

There has never been a perfect news source, one that didn't ramble, one that didn't interpolate with the odd 'umm' and 'ahh', one that didn't speak in half sentences. For example, what do you do about the news source whose subjects never agree with their verbs? If there were a perfect news source, then there would never be the temptation or necessity to clean up quotes (Germer 1995).

While there are no fixed rules, the following points of guidance about altering quotes from interviews are useful:

* You may wish to fix grammatical errors and correct syntax, and delete 'umming' and 'ahhing'.
* In most circumstances it is better to paraphrase than make someone look stupid because they have been quoted

literally. However, there may be times when it is appropriate
to quote even if the news source will suffer embarrassment.

- Never change quotes so that the meaning conveyed is
  different to that intended by the news source.
- It ~~can be~~ dangerous to add material to quotes.
- It can be dangerous to delete material from quotes.
- Watch slang and abbreviated language.
- Ensure that you are alert to racist, sexist and defamatory
  quotes from news sources. It will be no defence to say you
  quoted the source accurately! *In the U.S, this might be part of the story.*

Many journalists new to the profession believe that
because a defamatory statement has been quoted, they
are not liable. This is not true. Both the journalist and
their organisation can be sued for defamation as the
publishers of the statement.

Not in the U.S.

BEWARE MIXING AND MATCHING QUOTES

A trap for reporters is to take quotes from previously published
or broadcast material and import them into current stories.
Extra caution is needed if your feature story on a controversial
doctor contains six paragraphs of quotes, two taken from an
interview given five years ago, two quotes taken from yesterday's taped interview and two quotes taken from last week's
telephone interview—put together as a seamless flow as if the
source was speaking yesterday. This type of quote collage can
lead to distortion.

For example, the Australian Press Council upheld a complaint by the National Front of Australia against a Sunday
newspaper that quoted the Front's chairman saying, 'We have
been well trained in the use of guns and explosives if we

have to defend ourselves against political opponents'. The Press Council established that the quoted remarks were a composite of remarks allegedly made by the chairman at various places and various times.

The paper was clearly at fault in presenting remarks as a direct quotation when this was not the case. The Press Council said readers were entitled to believe that direct quotes were what they purported to be and censured the paper (Adjudication No. 55 1979).

MAKING IT UP

One thing that you should never do is to fabricate quotes. The New Zealand Press Council censored *New Truth* over a complaint by the Prostitutes' Collective following an article in which the paper attributed a quote to a particular woman. In her complaint the woman said she had not been interviewed and the words were not hers, and they were not the words of anyone else from her organisation. The editor said a freelance reporter had produced the story and had assured the paper that the comments attributed to the woman were accurate but had come from another member of the collective who asked, as a matter of protocol, that they be attributed to the woman as co-ordinator. The Press Council said the newspaper had attributed a quote to the woman but it now acknowledged it was not hers.

'At best this can be seen as a foolhardy lapse likely to cause distress to the individual involved and threaten the reputation of newspapers generally. The attribution of quotes which had not been made can be regarded only as disreputable journalism and reprehensible in the extreme' (New Zealand Press Council 1999: 26).

Stockwell and Scott, authors of the *All-Media Guide to Fair and Cross-Cultural Reporting*, believe it's important that when 'people are claiming some authority to speak on behalf of others, be sure that such authority has some basis in reality' and also 'be sure to determine when someone is speaking as an individual and when that person is speaking on behalf of a group or organization' (2000: 19).

SWEARING—EXPLETIVE DELETED OR EXPLETIVE REPORTED?

What happens in an interview when a public figure lets down their guard and swears? Should you report profanity, obscenity or swearing or not? Should you protect public figures from themselves when they swear? There are no set answers to these questions. Whether to delete or report expletives depends on:

- what sort of publication or broadcaster you work for,
- the context in which the swearing occurs,
- who says it,
- commonly accepted standards of decency and good taste, and
- whether the expletive adds something essential to the story.

What is acceptable for one publisher or broadcaster may be unacceptable for another. Even within daily journalism there is often a division of opinion over whether to report swearing. In a celebrated New Zealand case, half the daily media reported Health Minister Annette King's swear words when she was telephoned in Brisbane in the middle of the night and asked about allegations that she'd gone on an overseas 'honeymoon' at taxpayers' expense. The other half of the news media, including Radio New Zealand and the Press Association, did not report the swearing. Venting her anger at the late night allegations, Mrs King said on the telephone, 'This just pisses me off. I've worked bloody hard, I've had one day off'. The incident reverberated for at least a week in letters to the editor, in cartoons and on talkback radio. For example D.J. Aitchison wrote in *The Dominion*, 'I was appalled at the foul language used by Health Minister Annette King. A mouthwash is definitely needed—unless such coarse words are normal for Labor members of Parliament' (2 June 2000: 2).

The Health Minister was forced to apologise for using swear words. 'I have never been known to swear in public. It was uncharacteristic and I feel I let myself down' (Brockett 2000: 1), which are all good quotes in themselves.

Some guidance to commonly accepted standards of decency and good taste comes from the information produced by bodies such as the Australian Broadcasting Authority and the New Zealand Broadcasting Standards Authority, which monitor trends in public taste and regularly publish lists of the acceptability and unacceptability of bad language in broadcasting (Dickinson, Hill & Zwaga 2000).

Cartoon courtesy of the cartoonist, Jim Hubbard.

JUDGEMENT CALLS

Other judgements reporters must make in using interview material involve whether the information given to you was 'on the record' or 'off the record', and how to check the accuracy of what was said. You need to be aware that different stories may call for different judgements and that different media have specific rules or practices that may not be universal. For example, some newsrooms do not allow you to use anonymous sources, unless the journalist is experienced and there is confidence in the source. In broadcasting, however, paraphrasing someone's comments so the audience doesn't know the source of the news is common.

You should also keep in mind that some issues such as the use of anonymous sources and whether stories should be checked back with interviewees are subject to a good deal of healthy and critical debate in journalism generally. For example, the O.J. Simpson case generated so many stories based on anonymous sources that *Los Angeles Daily News* writer Ray Richmond satirically suggested setting up a 'Rent-a-Source' service for reporters (Shepard 1994).

ANONYMOUS SOURCES

The use of anonymous sources is a hot topic in journalism. There are those who insist the use of named sources is critical to the purpose and credibility of journalism. They argue that not to name sources devalues the news and leads to lower journalistic standards. Public trust in news reporting is damaged if people can't see and hear who is being quoted. Some journalists believe using unnamed sources leads to lazy journalism and allows politicians and public officials to take 'cheap shots' against opponents under the veil of anonymity.

Defenders of anonymous sources on the other hand, including Watergate reporter Bob Woodward, believe some important stories would never surface without them. Woodward says unnamed sources can be a valuable tool.'The job of a journalist, particularly someone who's spent time dealing in sensitive areas, is to find out what really happened' (Shepard 1994). He says there is no way of reporting on the inside of agencies like the CIA, Pentagon or the White House without using anonymous sources, because people won't necessarily go on the record. The Australian Press Council says 'the quoting of anonymous sources is common and justifiable practice in political reporting' (Adjudication No. 55 1979).

TIPS: ON NAMING SOURCES

1. Treasure the value of named sources that give your stories credibility.
2. Only use confidential sources for very important information.
3. Always verify information from confidential sources with another source.
4. Don't allow sources to go 'off the record' unless there are exceptional circumstances.
5. Know what 'off the record' means. It does not mean you can't use the information if you can get it elsewhere, but it does mean you can't attribute the information to the news source who has given it to you on an 'off the record' basis.
6. Never betray a confidential source. However, you may have to disclose the identity of unnamed sources on a confidential basis to your superior.

7. You must always question the motives of unnamed sources.
8. Be particularly cautious about unnamed sources who express opinions about others or who are judgemental.
9. Readers, listeners and viewers should be told why a source's identity is not being disclosed.
10. Beware the anonymous source who is only available on the telephone and can't be traced—never trust information from anonymous sources you've never met.

Never bow to pressure to name confidential sources. The Australian Press Council says 'it is a principle well established in journalism, and one which the Press Council habitually upholds, that sources of information published in newspapers are not to be inquired into' (Adjudication No. 39 1978). Australian and New Zealand journalists are staunch defenders of the principle of non-disclosure in controversial cases and have been prepared to risk prison in contempt of court cases.

HONOURING THE DEAL

Some stories involve reporters agreeing to the terms under which the interview will be conducted and how the material will be published or broadcast. Very often this is a confusing area for members of the public who have little experience of the news media. It can also be difficult for reporters. The deals you make on the spot to get the story may, in fact, contradict your newsroom policy or the protocols of the broadcaster or publication you are working for. A process of negotiation then begins.

Most reporters abide by the convention that once they have established their identity and the organisation they work for on the telephone or face-to-face with a news source or interviewee, then anything the interviewee says from that point can legitimately be reported. Many news organisations have a 'no deals' policy and believe that proper sourcing and attribution establishes the credibility of news. However some cases are not so clear-cut. Take the following situation in which the man interviewed felt he had made an agreement with the reporter that he be referred to as a 'family source' but not named.

The story concerned the behaviour of two boys from well-to-do families who went on a rampage of arson. One of the fathers was interviewed and quoted at some length in the story. He had no objection to this because he felt his experience might help other parents but he did not wish to be personally identified. The father said he made it perfectly clear to the reporter that he was speaking on the condition that he was not named. The reporter said that she would have to refer to a higher authority in the newsroom to see if his comments could be published anonymously, in keeping with the paper's policy.

The deputy editor contacted the father and said the paper could not agree to his request for anonymity and the article would be published the next day using both his name and comments. Although the father objected that he had only agreed to be interviewed if his name was not used, the story was published quoting him by name, listing his profession and place of work. The story was a good piece of journalism and the name of the father as its source added to the story's credibility. But the New Zealand Press Council said the father was entitled to expect the newspaper to honour the basis on which he agreed to be interviewed. 'A newspaper cannot unilaterally impose its own rules upon a member of the public while choosing to ignore any conditions he may have set' (1999: 64).

SHOW AND TELL?

An unwritten taboo in journalism is showing or reading back a story before publication to a news source. Showing what you've written can allow the source an opportunity to meddle with your story. Sources may want to alter the tone or emphasis as a consequence. Readbacks also take time and threaten deadlines. Again there is a wide division of opinion in journalism about the practice. On the one hand it has been called a 'moronic practice' that relegates reporters to glorified secretaries. On the other hand, readbacks are standard practice and called the 'accuracy check' at the *Missourian*, the paper run by the University of Missouri School of Journalism in Columbia (Shepard 1996).

It is best to follow local rules about showing a story to a news source after the interview and before publication. While read backs are not normally done there may be some exceptional circumstances in which you choose to show back quotes. These include:

- reassuring yourself that you got it right,
- reassuring a source who is innocent of the media's ways,
- ensuring complex, technical subjects in science, technology or business are correctly reported, and
- building trust with an important but reluctant source.

Another technique might be to read back the interviewee's quotes before you leave the interview. This protects you in terms of accuracy but does not damage journalistic integrity.

THE USE OF TAPED TELEPHONE CONVERSATIONS

Some reporters tape all telephone conversations as an insurance policy. They follow the practice whether the person at the other end is aware of the taping or not. In New Zealand it is not unlawful for any person to tape a conversation with another and a secretly recorded conversation is admissible in court. Former Prime Minister Robert Muldoon, for example, taped all media interviews and often used the tape recordings to allege that he had been misreported. Imagine the effect this had on young journalists when this formidable politician began an interview by deliberately and elaborately setting up his microphone and ostentatiously turning on his equipment.

However, the reporter's right to use taped telephone conversations is not unlimited. New Zealand's Broadcasting Standards Authority (BSA) upheld a complaint that TV3 broadcast a taped conversation between a criminal lawyer and a reporter after the journalist had given an assurance of confidentiality. The case was an unusual one because the criminal lawyer was hawking the story from a controversial Maori politician and asking the network for $20 000 for an exclusive interview. The broadcaster said the story involving a chequebook journalism request was of such public interest that it justified the network breaking the confidence. The BSA said it was concerned with the concept of fairness under-pinning broadcasting standards. Playing part of a tape of a conversation as a news item, recorded after an assurance of confidentiality had been given, was unfair. The lawyer had good grounds to assume that the conversation was confidential. Because of this he was less guarded than he might otherwise have been and thus a degree of entrapment was involved in the subsequent conversation (BSA 1997, Decision No. 129).

REFERENCES

Aitchison, D.J. 2000, 'Mouthwash needed', *The Dominion*, Letters page, 2 June 2000, p. 2

Australian Broadcasting Authority Website: www.aba.gov.au

Australian Press Council 1977, Adjudication No. 9, March 1977, http://www.austlii.edu.au/cgi-bin/disp.pl/au/other/apc/9.html?query=%7e+quote

—— 1978, Adjudication No. 39, October 1978, http://www.austlii.edu.au/cgi-bin/disp.pl/au/other/apc/39.html?query=%7e+source

—— 1979, Adjudication No. 55, May 1979, http://www.austlii.edu.au/cgi-bin/disp.pl/au/other/apc/55.html?query=%7e+source

—— 1999, Adjudication No. 1057, November 1999, http://www.austlii.edu.au/au/other/apc/1057.html?query=%7e+adjudication+no+1057

Broadcasting Standards Authority 1997, Decision No. 129, http://www.bsa.govt.nz

Brockett, M. 2000, 'Blushing bride sorry for swearing in public', *The Dominion*, 2 June 2000, p. 1

Cappon, R.J. 1982, *The Word: An Associated Press Guide to Good News Writing*, Associated Press, New York

Dickinson, G., Hill, M. & Zwaga, Z. 2000, *Monitoring Community Attitudes in Changing Mediascapes*, Broadcasting Standards Authority, Wellington

Germer, F. 1995, 'Are quotes sacred?', *American Journalism Review*, September, pp. 34–7

Knowles, E. (ed.) 1998, *The Oxford Dictionary of 20th Century Quotations*, Oxford University Press, New York

New Zealand Press Council 1999, *The Twenty-seventh Report of the New Zealand Press Council*, New Zealand Press Council, Wellington

Personal interview with Dr Brian Edwards, October 2000

Personal interview with Kerry O'Brien, November 2000

Shepard, A.C. 1994, 'Anonymous sources', *American Journalism Review*, December, pp. 20–5

—— 1996, 'Show and print', *American Journalism Review*, March, pp. 40–4

Stockwell, S. and Scott, P. 2000, *All-Media Guide To Fair and Cross-Cultural Reporting*, Australian Key Centre for Cultural and Media Policy, Nathan, Queensland

10

KEEPING SAFE

The news gathering interview involves journalists in situations where there are legal and ethical consequences. As a reporter it is important to develop intuitive antennae that will alert you to legal and ethical concerns when interviewing. But you are not on your own. Remember different media organis- ations make judgements about ethical dilemmas and legal risks all the time, and you can ask for advice from colleagues and news superiors. In this chapter we use a drugs scenario as the background to explore issues about media law and reporters' ethics to help you think about some of the inter- view contexts involved.

SCENARIO

A reporter notices from reading the obituary columns an unusual number of death notices for young teenagers in the same month. She makes inquiries of a friendly police source and finds the deaths are heroin overdoses, and all the teenagers are from the same school. The source also tells her

that one of the dead youngsters is related to a prominent tele-
vision personality, and there are rumours that the TV star
introduced the teenagers to cannabis before they graduated to
heroin. Her police contact reluctantly tells her in confidence
that a major heroin cartel is operating between Australia and
New Zealand, and the deaths are related to one shipment. The
police reporter, Jane Light, asks her police contact if she can
talk to her editor in confidence about the information. Her
editor agrees that she can work on the story in her own time,
but to report back to the newsroom with any developments.
As Jane makes more inquiries she finds a lot of little pieces
emerging. In interviews with relatives of the dead teenagers,
the TV personality's name is mentioned several times. One
parent said the TV star was always present at parties attended
by his son.'I suspect he introduced my boy to hard drugs,' he
said. A women's magazine featured a cover story with the TV
star distraught at the graveside of the man's dead son. There
are also rumours of police corruption. Several prominent
business people are alleged to be laundering drug money.

Privacy

Jane decides to start her investigation by interviewing friends
and family of the young teenagers who've died of drug overdoses. There is wide public interest in preventing heroin abuse
in the community and Jane believes her readers need to know
what's happening. She realises this is a sensitive time to call
grieving family and friends. She will rehearse her opening
before telephoning or visiting the families, but is aware she
might be rebuffed. When she calls she will pay her condolences
and ask gently but persuasively for an interview. Jane believes
by interviewing the families the publicity may act as a deter-
rent, and she may pick up information for her wider
investigation into the drug cartel.

How many times can a reporter telephone and request an interview?

First, Jane will have to take into account the general ethical presumption that grieving families should be treated with dignity, compassion and respect. For example the free-to-air broadcasting code charges New Zealand television reporters with avoiding unnecessary intrusion in the grief and distress of victims and their families or friends. The New Zealand Press Council's Statement of Principles states that 'those suffering from trauma or grief call for special consideration, and when approached, or enquiries are being undertaken, careful attention is to be given to their sensibilities' (1999: 16–17). The Australian Code of Ethics, developed by the Media, Entertainment and Arts Alliance (MEAA), covers similar ground in Code No. 11 which states that journalists should 'Respect private grief and personal privacy. Journalists have the right to resist compulsion to intrude' (1999, http://www.alliance.org.au).

Second, Jane should know that merely telephoning someone once or twice or visiting their home seeking legitimate information will not constitute a nuisance. However, harassment by persistent telephone calls or badgering relatives unnecessarily is another story. In an unusual New Zealand case, a newspaper publisher was found guilty of misusing a telephone by making annoying calls to victims of a rafting tragedy on the pretext of a journalistic inquiry (Burrows & Cheer 1999). Even though he'd been given a clear message not to call back after the first call he made three calls to one victim. In the Australian context, Pearson states that 'continuous telephone calls, persisting despite requests that they cease, could be considered a nuisance, while a series of phone calls merely seeking an interview for a story would not normally be considered as such' (1997: 226).

Despite her motive for seeking a compelling story that

might prevent further drug deaths, Jane needs to be aware that she is still intruding at a time of grief, and that it is rare that anyone who has just lost a loved one will welcome the attention. She had heard rumours of one television journalist who had turned up at the home of one of the families and could not understand why his offer of a box of iced donuts was not accepted as entrée into the grieving parents' home. Jane knows that the hardest interviews reporters have to undertake involve death and grief. Some reporters are better at these interviews than others, but even experienced journalists find them tough.

Deathknocks, as they are called (see Chapter 1), involve telephoning or approaching grieving family members or friends about a person who has died immediately after the death. There is no easy way to undertake deathknocks. Such interviews require courage and sensitivity. Reporters face a range of reactions in asking to speak with families in times of grief. Some people are adamantly opposed to any intrusion whatsoever and are angry at the approach. Others welcome the reporter as someone to talk to, for the opportunity to publicise something they feel is wrong, and to acknowledge a loved one.

Deathknocks

Jane knows from media coverage of the Port Arthur massacre in Tasmania in 1996, when 35 people were shot dead, that ordinary people can be thrust into the media limelight despite their right to 'private grief'. She has been reading *To Have and to Hold*, Walter Mikac's book co-authored with Lindsay Simpson, detailing the tragic loss of his wife and two daughters who were shot and killed in the massacre. A friend of Walter's wife, Lindsay was working for the *Sydney Morning Herald* at the time and had been sent to cover the massacre. Reluctantly she contacted the Mikac home where the phone was answered by the family doctor. When she explained that the call was part of her work for the *Herald* and not a personal call, the doctor replied by asking whether she thought that Walter had the right to grieve in private. She agreed that he did, and ended the call.

But as Jane knows, not all the media dealt with the case so ethically or responsibly. The media attention was immediate for Walter and the other victims. On trying to enter the Port Arthur historic site the day after the massacre, Walter saw a 'huge contingent of vehicles, police milling around and people standing behind an impromptu barricade'. He said:

> The media line acted like a starting line rather than a barricade. Bodies with microphones and cameras surged towards our vehicle. I didn't want to be photographed like this, but then again I wanted the world to see the tears that were welling up in every cell of my body. I could hear the shutters flickering. At that moment I knew that I was no longer just a husband and father mourning the loss of his life's essence—whether I liked it or not, I had become one of the living casualties, the walking wounded from Port Arthur. The image of my distressed, slumped body trying to deny the inevitable would be splashed all over the newspapers the following day (Mikac & Simpson 1997: 5–6).

Jane is aware that some organisations today are advocating different approaches to deathknocks—one, to use an intermediary to talk to the media (such as a counsellor), and another, to have just one journalist conduct the interview which can then be disseminated to the rest of the media. In a case where a three-year-old girl was abducted and killed by a fourteen-year-old boy early in 2001, the local chaplain represented the family in dealings with the media. In Mikac's case, he said:

I also had to tackle the strange experience of being a celebrity—for which I had no training and no time to prepare. The media wanted a piece of the action now. I was newsworthy and deadlines could not wait . . . But on the Tuesday after the shooting, I decided I would speak to Ray Martin on 'A Current Affair'. If the media train was approaching, I was going to meet it head on. I could dictate the terms. I would speak once and that was it (Mikac & Simpson 1997: 135).

Jane knows that quotes from family members are highly newsworthy when young people have tragically died of drug abuse, so how does she reconcile the wider public interest with the right of personal privacy?

She refers to the Victims' Task Force *Training Kit for Journalists* (1993) for general principles. These and other pointers are included here.

1. Use a neutral third party like a police officer, family friend or funeral director to make the first approach.
2. It is legitimate to ask whether there is someone in the family who would like to pay tribute to the dead person.
3. Persuasion but not compulsion is the tactic that secures the best result.
4. If the family declines an interview that should be the end of the approach although the reporter can leave a card or a contact number should the family change its mind.
5. If during an interview a family member becomes upset or wishes to exit, the reporter should acknowledge the rights of the interviewee.
6. Ensure that during the interview the reporter does not reveal sensitive or upsetting information that may have been concealed from the family by the police or other authorities.

7. Request photos of the dead person only at the end of the interview and after you have built an empathetic relationship with the interviewee.

8. Funerals are not generally the best times for the first approach because they are highly charged with emotion and grief.

9. Be aware that the interviewee is grieving and may regret the revelations when they are published or broadcast. Not all family members will welcome the publicity.

The Victims' Task Force *Training Kit* was produced after thirteen people died in a tragic slaying by gunman David Gray, at the tiny South Island hamlet of Aramoana. If Jane was working in New Zealand, she would have to be aware of Maori feelings about insensitive interviewing about death and tragedy. A Maori freelance journalist, Queenie Rikihana Hyland, says 'to Maori the three days of a tangi (tangihanga—ceremony of mourning) give relief spiritually, emotionally and physically'. She suggests the media need to leave suffering families alone to get on with their grieving within their whanau (extended family). 'In this way caring and help for the "victims" who survive will not end at the graveside and with the immediate "news story" but will go on for as long as they are needed' (1992: 7). Michael King in his guide to reporting Maori activities has this advice: 'the message here is one that has been stressed already: where there is a cultural gap to cross, you have to do more leg-work to win people's confidence and display more sensitivity towards the feelings of your subjects. In the process, you will not only produce a less offensive story—you will get a better one' (1985: 32–3). There are also restrictions on reporting the death of an Elder in an Aboriginal community. The most important point for Jane to remember is that they should not name the deceased.

Off the record

After two unsuccessful attempts to speak to the parents of some of the dead youngsters, Jane hears that the father who told her about the TV star is willing to talk to her again—but only if some of the information is 'off the record'. After speaking to her editor, who agrees to the conditions, the interview is set up at his house. While Jane is conducting the interview she notices some family photographs (as does the photographer who is with her). While the father is out of the room answering the phone, the photographer urges Jane to take one of the photos, but she refuses. She asks the father some personal questions, but when he declines to answer them, she does not persist. As promised, the story the next day is about the drugs issue, but the headline has been sensationalised compared to the story written by Jane. It reads: 'Heroin death destroys local family', which in no way reflects the content of the story. She complains to the editor, and decides to call the father to apologise. Unfortunately he decides he will no longer deal with Jane because of the story's treatment.

Investigative journalism

Jane is troubled by the sensationalism. She has learned that journalism involves tensions between newsroom decisions and her own personal feelings about building trust with people she interviews. She decides to keep on digging and interviewing others to get the drugs story. She is inspired by examples of journalistic tenacity. Prize-winning Kiwi investigative journalist Warren Berryman defines investigative journalism as 'an attitude of mind towards a story so that you never leave something that begs the question why . . . the investigative journalist will keep on niggling away' (quoted in Booth 1992: 162). Investigative journalist Chris Masters, of ABC's 'Four Corners', describes investigative journalism as a 'big dig'. He says despite the considerable resources of the media, the big dig happens all too infrequently. A big dig can improve public perceptions about an important issue virtually overnight. He adds, however, that a big dig can take up to three months to complete at some pain to colleagues and bosses (Masters 1992: 15–16).

During the first interview Jane receives some possible leads regarding the heroin deaths, and requests time to do some more research. The newsroom is quite large and fully staffed (with no-one away on leave) so the editor reluctantly agrees to give her a few days. Jane is pleased to have even this small amount of time granted. She decides to do another library search first, and talk to the police reporter, before heading out.

Anonymous sources and contempt of court

Jane goes back to the original source of information (the obituaries) and also looks through file copies of local papers, including her own. She finds several stories on drug raids conducted by police, with the names of two officers appearing frequently in these stories. Jane decides these names are her next lead, though she is unsure how much help will be provided regarding her investigations.

Both officers refuse to talk to Jane when she phones and suggest she contact the police media liaison officer. She does, but again runs into a brick wall. Several days later, however, she is contacted by her friendly police source who has heard talk around the station that she is still investigating heroin deaths. They agree to meet in a small suburban coffee shop on the opposite side of the city to the police station. Her source asks for complete anonymity. The MEAA Code of Ethics points out that 'where a source seeks anonymity, do not agree without first considering the source's motives and any alternative attributable sources. Where confidences are accepted, respect them in all circumstances'. The New Zealand Press Council's Statement of Principles states that 'editors have a strong obligation to protect against disclosure of the identity of confidential sources. They also have a duty to take reasonable steps to satisfy themselves that such sources are well informed and that the information they provide is reliable'. Broadcasters too are obliged to monitor the integrity of their sources.

Jane agrees to his request and decides to meet him, but tells her editor where she is going, and the time she thinks the interview will take. Jane knows that if this case ever goes before the courts, she could be charged with contempt of court (perhaps even gaoled) for withholding the name of the source, but she is willing to do this to get the story. However, if she breaks the trust it would not only damage her reputation, but also that of investigative journalists generally. On talking to the police officer Jane learns that a small number of police are involved in covering for heroin traders, some connected to local businessmen. Her friendly police source is alarmed at police corruption but does not want to betray his colleagues. Jane believes he is genuine and that she has a 'big story'.

Jane now has to independently corroborate the source's information so she can honour her promises of anonymity and confidentiality to her friendly policeman. He had given her two names of people he was sure would help—one a fellow 'honest cop' who also wanted to remain anonymous, the other a relative of one of the dead teenagers. She knows this will be a good start, and hopefully lead to other sources to confirm the police officer's story. At this point the relative is the only person willing to go on the record.

What if they won't answer?

Jane goes back to her editor and tells him what she has found. She requests more time. He too can sense it is a big story and grants her another week. Jane knows she will have to put in a lot of overtime even with this extension. She is also concerned with what could happen if no-one will answer her questions, and she comes away from these two interviews empty handed.

As a relatively new reporter, Jane needs to develop her own style. Here is how an experienced journalist like Chris Masters describes his approach.

> There are few worse setbacks than an exclusive witness's firm refusal to talk. I have, in my time, sweated over many a telephone. There is no technique that guarantees success . . . All I can say is it helps to be honest. When a journalist calls, people's bullshit detectors are instantly turned on. It is also worth remembering there is no long-term profit in deceiving a witness. If you do end up in court, you want them as friends, not enemies. I find it also helps to be curious. Everybody has a story to tell and there is a frequent compulsion to tell it. Some of the best 'investigative' journalists are, quite simply, good listeners (Masters 1992: 48–9).

Establishing credibility and chequebook journalism

Jane is not concerned about the validity of information from the 'honest cop', but is concerned about the information she might receive from the relative of someone who died of drug abuse. When she first contacts the relative, he asks how much the newspaper will be paying for the story.

The controversial issue of chequebook journalism currently bedevils the news media. It is a common practice in women's magazines, tabloid journalism and in commercial television, but seldom occurs on community newspapers, such as Jane's, nor on Radio New Zealand, the ABC or SBS.

Chris Masters says: 'Chequebook journalism is a common, unattractive feature of the profession. If you pay a witness for a story the evidence is immediately devalued, certainly in the eyes of the courts. The theory is that witnesses who work for reward might be encouraged to say anything. Even worse, they might be persuaded by a larger sum to later reverse their story' (Masters 1992: 58).

Jane persuades the relative he could be discredited in the community if it became known that he had profited from the tragedy.

Reputation and defamation

Jane decides to follow up on the parents' claims about the TV star who apparently introduced their children to heroin. In this section we look at some of the issues journalists need to be cautious about when interviewing to avoid defamation. The first tip for Jane is to know something about what defamation is. This allows her to identify the potential defamation when she is conducting interviews. Reporters are not expected to be experts and there is no single definition of defamation, which makes it a difficult area. Remember, however, that ignorance of defamation is no protection. Jane should at least know that defamation is about:

- injuring someone's reputation by publishing or broadcasting a false statement, and/or
- lowering the opinion of the person in the eyes of ordinary people, and/or
- bringing the person into hatred, ridicule or contempt, and/or
- saying something about someone that tends to make others shun or avoid them.

If Jane uses the father's quote that, 'I suspect he introduced my son to hard drugs', would the quote be defamatory? First, for the TV star to sue for defamation he would have to prove that the publication referred to him. Australian magnate Kerry Packer successfully sued for defamation despite only being referred to as 'the goanna'. Obviously if the TV star was named that would be identification. In this case he wasn't named. But the TV star could claim that the published statement refers to a small group of people, local TV stars, of whom he is a representative. How many TV stars are enough? As Pearson states, 'the courts have decided to view such cases in terms of the size of the class being defamed, the generality of the charges made and the extravagance of the accusation, with each case according to its circumstances. The test is whether ordinary, reasonable individuals would believe the defamatory statements referred to the plaintiffs' (1997: 108). Burrows and Cheer note that 'a statement that "all the lawyers in the town of X are incompetent sharks", there being only four lawyers in that town, would ground a defamation action by each of the four' (1999: 38).

So what if Jane quotes the father as making the statement? Is she safe? No. Jane does not have a defence simply because she is quoting someone else's words. Nor does it matter if Jane didn't intend to defame the TV star, she is still liable. It will not help the reporter, either, that she was merely reporting a suspicion or a rumour. The reporter has to prove the rumour was true, not just that there were rumours around about the TV star and drugs.

So how can Jane report the TV star's alleged involvement? Can she put the rumours to him and report his response? Burrows and Cheer warn against such a strategy. 'A defamatory rumour coupled with a denial of a rumour might still leave the matter capable of a defamatory meaning' (1999: 27). It is dangerous to use the device, 'TV star X today denied rumours that he introduced teenagers to hard drugs following the deaths of several youths from overdoses', because some ordinary readers, listeners or viewers may suspect he did.

The best way for Jane to defend herself against a defamation action is to prove the TV star introduced teenagers to hard drugs. Remember if it comes to court the TV star does not have to prove he didn't, the reporter has to prove he did. Truth as a defence is based on the notion that a person's reputation is based on actions and behaviour and that publication of the truth merely broadcasts the reputation to a wider audience (Pearson 1997). If the journalist does have proof then there is clear public interest in exposing a public figure who is involved in the distribution of drugs.

Jane has conducted dozens of interviews in her investigation and feels frustrated that she cannot write her big story. She spends several hours with the relative and publishes a specific story about his knowledge of the parties where teenagers were using drugs. After the story is published a school friend of the dead boy telephones Jane and tells her the TV star had also offered him heroin at a party. He says he is prepared to tell his parents and have a story written so no other friends die.

Jane tells her editor, who contacts the paper's lawyer. The lawyer suggests Jane interview the boy with his parents present and show them back her copy before publication (an exception to the paper's policy).

Jane has a scoop—a story that is both of public interest and in the public interest. She has succeeded through luck, persistence, building trust and effective interviewing.

Remember that more experienced journalists such as your chief reporter, editor or news manager have first-hand experience of tricky interview situations. Always keep them informed and take early advice about legal and ethical matters. It can save painful apologies, damaged journalistic reputations and expensive payouts. Keep them informed of all your dealings with interviewees that may have ethical or legal ramifications. Many organisations also have legal advisors and trainers who can provide guidance and help to check work if you are unsure.

REFERENCES

Booth, P. 1992, 'Investigative journalism: the New Zealand experience', in *Whose News?*, eds M. Comrie and J. McGregor, Dunmore Press, North Palmerston, pp. 161-9

Burrows, J. & Cheer, U. 1999, *Media Law in New Zealand*, 4th edn, Oxford University Press, Auckland

Butler, D. & Rodrick, S. 1999, *Australian Media Law*, LBC Information Services, New South Wales

Hyland, Q.R. 1992, 'Healing after tragedy', *Listener* and *TV Times*, 12 September 1992, p. 7

King, M. 1985, *Kawe Korero—A guide to Reporting Maori Activities*, New Zealand Journalists Training Board, Wellington

Masters, C. 1992, *Inside Story*, Angus & Robertson, Sydney

Media, Entertainment and Arts Alliance 1999, 'Code of Ethics' http://www.alliance.org.au

Mikac, W. and Simpson, L. 1997, *To Have and To Hold: A Modern-Day Love Story Cut Short*, Macmillan, Sydney

New Zealand Press Council 1999, 'Statement of Principles', *The 27th Report of the New Zealand Press Council*, Wellington

Pearson, M. 1997, *The Journalist's Guide to Media Law*, Allen & Unwin, Sydney

Victims' Task Force 1993, *Victims of Crime*, A Training Kit for Journalists, Wellington

RESOURCES

AUSTRALIA

Access to the Information and Services of the Australian, Federal, State and Territory Governments   http://www.gov.au
A long and unwieldy title, but this site provides very easy access to information from around Australia, with links to agencies, departments and specific personnel.

Associations on the Net   http://www.ipl.org/ref/AON
The Internet Public Library Associations on the Net (AON) provide more than 2000 sites covering professional and trade associations, as well as research institutions. The site is divided into easily located subject areas such as business and economics.

Australian Bureau of Statistics   http://www.abs.gov.au
Australia's official statistical service, offering publications, spreadsheets and detailed information on areas including health, expenditure, exchange rates and industry.

Australian Commonwealth Government Entry Point
http://www.fed.gov.au
This site provides easy links to government information, useful
and accessible background information on Australia's systems
of government and updates on 'Australia Now'. It also includes
a useful site map for tracking down information.

Australian Journalist Desktop
http://www.netspace.net.au/~moloney
A well-organised site with rounds—including politics and
health—quick links to phone numbers, experts, newsbreakers
and other useful Internet resources.

Australian News.net   http://australiannews.net
This site is particularly useful for the Headline News section,
but also provides links to rounds including rural news, finance
and sport.

Australian Newspapers on the Internet
http://www.nla.gov.au/oz/npapers.html
This very comprehensive site is produced by the National
Library of Australia and has direct links to the hundreds of
Australian newspapers produced online.

Forbes.com.People Tracker
http://beta.forbes.com/cms/template/peopletracker/index.jhtml
This site enables you to track more than 120 000 executives
and members of the Forbes rich and celebrity lists, as well
as research public companies. Best of all, subscription is
free!

Government On-Line Directory
http://gold.directory.gov.au.tmpl/s.html
An extremely useful site, this official guide to the Australian

Federal Government provides access to agencies, departments and government portfolios.

NEW ZEALAND

New Zealand Government Executive
http://www.executive.govt.nz or http://www.cabinet.govt.nz
Profiles of ministers, their speeches, press releases and news-letters are all available here. If you need to know the membership of a cabinet committee, this is the place to come. From this site, you can subscribe to a mailing list for ministerial press releases or speeches. (The speed of delivery really depends on the press secretary. You might find that the fax or a site such as Newsroom (http://www.newsroom.co.nz) is quicker.)

New Zealand Government Online   http://www.govt.nz
It's worth getting to know this site well. It's a gateway to all state sector Websites, including both central and local government. The 'agency contacts' button on the green banner at the top of the page takes you into a helpful division of the various government agencies, from departments to airports. This site will also help you find the Web address of government-ordered inquiries (which are now being given their own sites as soon as they are set up). See, for example, the Royal Commission on Genetic Modification at http://www.gmcommission.govt.nz.

New Zealand Legislation
http://www/gplegislation.co.nz/acts.html
If you want to check.something in an Act, this database can be browsed for free (Acts only, not Bills). If you want to use the search facility, however, rather than just browsing, you will have to pay.

NEW ZEALAND NEWS SITES

You can keep up with New Zealand news via the growing number of local Websites. Particularly useful are the *New Zealand Herald* at http://www.herald.co.nz and INL's aggregation of newspapers at Stuff (http://www.stuff.co.nz). These Websites do not have the same depth as commercial databases of newspaper content, but searches of the sites are free.

Television New Zealand's site is at http://www.nzoom.co.nz and TV3's at http://www.tv3.co.nz. Telecom's Internet Service Provider Xtra also runs a news site at http://www.xtra.co.nz. They have a handy link to Radio New Zealand, but you can access RNZ via http://www.rnz.co.nz (the sound) or http://www.radionz.co.nz (information about Radio New Zealand only).

Local Websites which started out by publishing media releases (and are still very good for media releases) are Newsroom (http://www.newsroom.co.nz) and Scoop (http://www.scoop.co.nz). They've expanded recently into broader news coverage of both New Zealand and, increasingly, world affairs.

Other handy Websites

Baycorp   http://www.baycorp.co.nz
For the traditional credit checks and much, much more, this paying site is indispensable for journalists. You can also use the Companies Office Website at http://www.companies.govt.nz where you can research partial company information for free and find out details such as banned directors. This site also houses the Motor Vehicles Securities Register and the National Insolvency Service.

Property information can be found on Quotable Value New Zealand Website at http://www.quotable.co.nz. The site's services are fee-based and there is a minimum charge of NZ$12 for casual users of the Infobase database.

Births, Deaths and Marriages can be found at http://www.bdm.govt.nz. You can apply for certificates via email.

The Elections Website (http://www.elections.org.nz) rolls three agencies into one—the Electoral Enrolment Centre, Chief Electoral Office and the Electoral Commission—and has a wealth of information. If you need to check out the registration of a political party, this is the place. On election night, official results are posted here. If you want to check electoral details you can do it here. (You need a name, date of birth and address details to use the online search facility.)

Browse Hansard for free at http://www.gplegislation.co.nz/hansard.html, although the transcripts are published here about ten to fourteen days later. You can browse as far back as 1987 but if you want to search for a particular entry you have to pay. For general information about parliament try http://www.parliament.govt.nz. To home in on the day's order paper or select committee hearings, ask the Clerk of the House at http://www.clerk.parliament.govt.nz.

The Website of the Australasian Legal Information Institute, a joint facility of UTS and UNSW Faculties of Law, contains a database of selected New Zealand Court of Appeal decisions released by the Court since 1998. You can find the New Zealand information at http://www.austlii.edu.au/nz/cases/NZCA.

For a selection of land information, try Land Information New Zealand at http://www.linz.govt.nz. Check out the Authoritative Streets and Places (ASP) database, searchable online. Input a street name and the database will tell you where it is and which electorate it's in. Select the 'databases' option on the site's home page to access the ASP and other databases.

You'll find a comprehensive site about the Waitangi Tribunal's work at http://www.waitangi-tribunal.govt.nz. You can also get free access to some parts of the Tribunal's reports but for the full text of the Waitangi Treaty, in Māori and English see the main government site at http://www.govt.nz/aboutnz/treaty.php3.

One of the most comprehensive New Zealand directories is located at the National Library's Website. The Te Puna Web Directory is a redevelopment of Ara Nui, which was started by Lincoln University. This directory, which has both New Zealand and Pacific Island Information, is at http://tepuna.natlib.govt.nz/web_directory. For Māori resources try Nga matatiki rorohiko: Māori Electronic Resources at http://www.auckland.ac.nz/lbr/maori/maorigate.htm. Some of the resources are available only to staff and students of Auckland University.

INDEX

Aborigines 44, 60
access 50-1
accidents 7
accuracy 25
actualities 114-15
aggression 7
Alysen, Barbara 2, 10, 131
amateurs 119-20
ambushes 4-5
anecdotes 108
angles 28-9, 45-6
annoyance 124
anonymity 152-4, 168-9
answers 115, 118-19
appointments 50
atmosphere 14
audio drop-in 3
avoidance 132-3

background information 3, 26-8, 108-9
Barber, Lynn 21, 43-4, 46
Berryman, Warren 167
Biagi, Shirley 74, 98
body language 18, 100
Booth, Pat 34
breathing exercises 129
Broadcasting Standards Authority (BSA) 4-5, 157

Cappon, Rene J. 45
Carson, Andrea 94, 136
catch phrases 47
celebrities 10-11, 104
CEOs 10
challenge 7-8
chequebook journalism 170-1
children 11-12
choices 77
clarification 78-9
clippings books 29-30, 127
closed questions 72

code of ethics 5, 11-12
computer files 29-30
computer interviews 32-4
computer-assisted research and reporting (CARR) 32-4
concentration 14-15
confidence 21-2, 47
consequence 71
contact book 38-9
contempt of court 168-9
control 92-3
conversations 2, 7, 44, 156-7
corruption 7
courtesy 57
credibility 21, 170-1
criminals 11
Cropp, Amanda 52
cultural sensitivities 44, 59-60
curiosity 16-17

daily rounds 6
Davis, Mark 130
Davis, Peter 12, 57, 65
deals 154-5
deathknocks 5-6, 38, 163-6
defamation 171-4
devil's advocate 82
Diana, Princess of Wales 1
disasters 7
Doogue, Geraldine 2, 16
doorstop interviews 4-5
Dorman, Clive 10-11
Dorner, Jane 136, 138, 139
dress 48-9
du Fresne, Karl 53

Edwards, Dr Brian 32, 117, 128, 143
electronic filing 30
email interviews 4, 17, 131, 135-40
emotion 2
enunciation 129

equipment 98-9, 105
ethics 160-74 *passim*
evasion 24
events 6-7
exclusives 6-7
experts 12
eye contact 13, 41, 126, 143

fabrication 149-50
face-to-face interviews 18, 132
fact fudging 24
Faine, Jon 7, 14, 18
familiarity 10-11
Filipina women 60
first impressions 56
focus 43-4, 92-3, 121
freezing 128-9
Friend, Cecilia 32

gatekeepers 50-1
general knowledge 62
general rounds 6
genres 7-9
Gosper, Kevan 8-9
grabs 2, 7-9, 121-3
Granato, Len 103, 106
guiding 120-1, 126-7, 128-9

Hamilton, John 60, 63
handshakes 57
hard news 3, 94-5, 96-102 *passim*,
    121-3
Hill, Kim 24, 122
Hill, Sharon 5
human interest 3, 95, 102-9
hunches 29
Hunt, Graham 33
Hyland, Queenie Rikihana 166
hypothetical questions 81

icebreaker questions 56-66 *passim*, 99,
    105, 134
immediacy 113
information: background 25-8, 108-9;

gathering 2, 6, 34, 44; ranking 77
innocents 11
intensity 112
interest 43
interviews: accessing 50-1; ambush
    4-5; audio drop-in 3; background 3;
    broadcast 110-30 *passim*; computer
    32-4; continuous 3; deathknock 5-6,
    38, 163-6; definition 2-3; doorstop
    4-5; early arrival 98; email 4, 17, 131,
    135-40; emotional 2; equipment
    98-9, 105; event 6-7; face-to-face
    18, 132; fact and opinion 3; feature 2;
    first impressions 56; flow 47; group
    6; guiding 120-1; hard news 3, 94-5,
    96-102 *passim*, 121-3; human
    interest 3, 95, 102-9; news 96-102
    passim, 160; point of 43-4; print
    94-109 *passim*; psyching up 37-8;
    radio 3; real time 138; requesting
    162-3; round 6-7; satellite 4, 17, 18;
    soft news 3, 94, 95, 123-7; soundbite
    3; styles 7-9; techniques 12-17; tele-
    phone 4, 17, 131-2, 133-5; terms
    154-5; time and place for 97, 104;
    time judgement 125-6; vox pops 4
intimacy 112
investigative journalism 34-5, 95,
    167-8
irritation 124
issues story 24

journalists: broadcast 10, 110-30;
    passim; chequebook 170-1; elec-
    tronic 4, 5; humble 26; investigative
    34-5, 95, 167-8; magazine 3; print 5;
    skills 9-12; styles 7-9; television 5;
    video 129-30
judgement 152

Kelly, Fran 112
keywords 46-8, 105
King, Annette 150
King, Michael 59, 166

libraries 30-1
listening 14-15, 100, 107, 117, 135
living treasures 31
Lyneham, Paul 83

managed events 6
Maori 44, 59, 166
Masters, Chris 167-8, 170-1
media conferences 4
media minders 52-4
Meyer, Philip 32
Mikac, Walter 163-4
misquoting 139, 145-7
Morrison, Al 3, 110, 112, 114, 119, 129
Muldoon, Sir Robert 37
mumbling 129

name dropping 61
negotiation 154-5
nervousness 38, 123-4
new media 33
news interviews 45-6, 96-102 passim,
  160
notepads 40, 42, 98, 105
notes 101-2, 109, 135

Oakes, Laurie 44
objectivity 61-2
O'Brien, Kerry 7-8, 12, 17, 25, 57, 69,
  70, 80, 82, 95, 111, 113, 121, 146
observations 107
off the record 167
open questions 73
opinion 2
organisation 48-9, 105

Pacific Island communities 59
patterns 24
persistence 50
phone phobia 38
politeness 57, 135
politicians 4, 9, 10
powers of observation 62-3
preparation 12, 14, 25-8, 38

print interviews 94-109 passim
privacy 161
projection 86-7
pronunciation 129
public relations practitioners 52-4

questions 46-8: and answers 115;
  avoiding 24; closed 72; comment 100;
  double-barrelled 90; easy 99, 107;
  embarrassing 22; essential 69; hard
  21-2, 82-5, 99, 101; 'how does it feel?'
  85-6; hypothetical 81; icebreaker 99,
  105, 134; informed 71; innocent 87-8;
  leading 88-9; 'must ask' 75-6; off-beat
  107-8; open 73; opening 124-5;
  opinion 100; organising 98; repeating
  79-81; rephrasing 79-81; short 74;
  simple 134-5; 'tell me about yourself'
  91; trick 89; 'who cares' 71-2, 100-1;
  Who, What, When, Where, Why and
  How 3, 23, 43, 69-70, 95, 100; writing
  down 68-9, 98
Quinn, Keith 115-16
quotes 142-50 passim

radio 3
rapport 58, 59, 105, 118
recorders 40-2
relationships 24
relevance 43
religions 44
repetition 78-81
reputation 171-4
research 104-5; icebreakers 60-2;
  investigative journalism 34-5, 95,
  167-8; reasons for 21-5; time for
  25-6, 97-8
researchers 32
respect 16-17
Rich, Carole 134, 136
Richardson, Ruth 142
Roces, Mina 60

satellite interviews 4, 17, 18

Saunders, John 29
scoops 6-7
scrapbooks 29
sensationalism 167
shorthand notes 40, 42
show and tell 156
silence 16
soft news 3, 94, 95, 123-7
sound 117
soundbites 2
sources 6, 9-12, 31, 104-5, 152-4
Spalding, Sally 21, 23, 27, 28
spin doctors 24, 53, 54
spontaneous events 6, 7
sports stars 10-11, 104
street surveys 4
summaries 76-8
Sumpter, Randy 53-4
surprise tactics 50
surroundings 63-5, 106
swearing 150-1

talking heads 10
Tankard, James 53-4
tape 114

tape recorders 156-7
technique 12-17
technology 17-18
telephone: conversations 156-7;
    interviews 4, 17, 131-2, 133-5;
    terror 38
Telford, Deborah 28
Tiffen, Rodney 53
time 25-8, 111-14
time judgement 125-6
timeliness 43
time-wasting 59
Torres Strait Islanders 44
trends 24
Trow, Richard 136

Urban, Andrew 13, 14, 17, 62-3, 65

videojournalism 129-30
voicers 115-16
vox pops 4

Wendt, Jana 76-7, 92
Woodward, Bob 153
wraps 116-17